BIBLE STUDY COMMENTARY

1 Timothy – James

$3.95

Bible Study Commentary

Timothy—James

RAYMOND BROWN

Scripture Union
130, City Road, London EC1V 2NJ

CHRISTIAN LITERATURE CRUSADE
Fort Washington, Pennsylvania 19034

© 1983 Scripture Union
130 City Road, London EC1V 2NJ

First published 1983

ISBN 0 86201 117 5 (UK)
     0 87508 174 6 (USA)

Phototypeset in Great Britain by
Input Typesetting Ltd., London SW19 8DR.

**Printed in Great Britain by
Ebenezer Baylis & Son Limited
The Trinity Press, Worcester, and London.**

General Introduction

The world-wide church in the last quarter of the twentieth century faces a number of challenges. In some places the church is growing rapidly and the pressing need is for an adequately trained leadership. Some Christians face persecution and need support and encouragement while others struggle with the inroads of apathy and secularism. We must come to terms, too, with the challenges presented by Marxism, Humanism, a belief that 'science' can conquer all the ills of mankind, and a whole range of Eastern religions and modern sects. If we are to make anything of this confused and confusing world it demands a faith which is solidly biblical.

Individual Christians, too, in their personal lives face a whole range of different needs – emotional, physical, psychological, mental. As we think more and more about our relationships with one another in the body of Christ and as we explore our various ministries in that body, as we discover new dimensions in worship and as we work at what it means to embody Christ in a fallen world, we need a solid base. And that base can only come through a relationship with Jesus Christ which is firmly founded on biblical truth.

The Bible, however, is not a magical book. It is not enough to say, 'I believe', and quote a few texts selected at random. We must be prepared to work with the text until our whole outlook is moulded by it. We must be ready to question our existing position and ask the true meaning of the word for us in our situation. All this demands careful study not only of the text but also of its background and of our culture. Above all it demands prayerful and expectant looking to the Spirit of God to bring the word home creatively to our own hearts and lives.

This new series of books has been commissioned in response to the repeated requests for something new to follow on from Bible Characters and Doctrines. It is now over ten years since the first series of Bible Study Books was produced and it is hoped that the new series will reflect the changes of the last ten years and bring the Bible text to life for a new generation of readers. The series has three aims:

1. To encourage regular, systematic personal Bible reading. Each volume is divided into sections ideally suited to daily use, and will normally provide material for three months (the exceptions being Psalms and 2 Corinthians-Galatians, four months, and Mark and Ezra-Job, two months). Used in this way the books will cover the entire Bible in five years. The comments aim to give background information and enlarge on the meaning of the text, with special reference to the contemporary relevance. Detailed questions of application are, however, often left to the reader. The questions for further study are designed to aid in this respect.

2. To provide a resource manual for group study. These books do not provide a detailed plan for week by week study. Nor do they present a group leader with a complete set of ready-made questions or activity ideas. They do, however, provide the basic biblical material and, in the questions for further discussion, they give starting points for group discussion.

3. To build into a complete Bible commentary. There is, of course, no shortage of commentaries. Here, however, we have a difference. Rather than look at the text verse by verse the writers examine larger blocks of text, preserving the natural flow of the original thought and observing natural breaks.

Writers have based their comments on the Revised standard version and some have also used the New International Version in some detail. The books can, however, be used with any version.

1 and 2 Timothy, Titus, Philemon: Introduction

The 'Pastoral' letters addressed to Timothy and Titus, Paul's colleagues in the work, indicate both the problems and resources of young ministers in the first century churches. Timothy served for a period at Ephesus, and Titus had been sent to the island of Crete. In both places the work seems to have been far from easy. It is clear from the letters that there were internal problems as well as external pressures. False teachers were creating serious difficulties for inexperienced leaders and Paul sends these letters to provide his younger partners with sound advice and strong encouragement. There is a constant insistence on 'sound teaching' as the essential basis for good living. The heretical teachers appear to have been 'gnostics' (from the Greek word, *gnōsis*, 'knowledge', 1 Tim. 6:20) of some kind or other. Such people maintained that unique spiritual insight was only imparted to a favoured few by means of specially acquired knowledge and by initiation into an exclusive circle of privileged adherents who alone were 'saved'. Note Paul's insistence that God longs for *all* to be saved, not a restricted spiritual élite (1 Tim. 2:4; 4:10; Titus 2:11). 'Gnostics' frequently maintained that those who are 'saved' consistently avoid all contact with 'matter' which was held to be intrinsically evil (compare 1 Tim. 4:4). Marriage relationships were either prohibited or regarded as unhelpful and degrading (compare 1 Tim. 4:3). Dietary laws were also enforced (1 Tim. 4:3–5; compare Col. 2:16). Teaching of this kind had not merely disturbed the tranquillity of the churches, but had created havoc and led to spiritual destruction (see 1 Tim. 1:19,20; 2 Tim. 1:15; 2:17,18). Members of gnostic sects frequently engaged in highly speculative notions and took a keen interest in myths and genealogies (see 1 Tim. 1:3,4; 4:7; 2 Tim. 4:4; Titus 3:9). Note that the age of this sort of thing has certainly not passed. Several modern cults and sects give attention to similar, profitless novelties. The gnostic teachers who were troubling these churches also appear to have had a clearly Jewish background (1 Tim. 1:6,7; Titus 1:14–16); some opponents were insisting on circumcision and a form of salvation by works (Titus 1:10). As John Stott has reminded us: 'A new generation of young Timothys is needed, who will guard the sacred deposit of the gospel, who are determined to proclaim it and prepared to suffer for it, and who will pass it on pure and uncorrupted to the generation which in due course will rise up to follow them.' Those who wish to study such introductory matters as date and authorship should look at John Stott's *Guard the Gospel* (IVP) and, for greater detail, Donald Guthrie's *New Testament Introduction* (IVP).

Notes on Gnosticism

When Paul and his colleagues proclaimed the apostolic gospel which had been entrusted to them, they did not preach in a doctrinal vacuum. Scores of 'counterfeit gospels' were propagated in the ancient world. False teachers were as active in the early Christian world as false prophets had been in Old Testament times (Jer. 6:13,14; 23:17–22). Christian believers were expected to test the message (1 John 4:1).

By the second century various heretical notions had become widely circulated throughout the Roman Empire and some of this weird teaching is sometimes described by the composite term 'gnosticism'. The word comes from the Greek word *gnostikos* ('one who has knowledge'). It is important to recognise that 'gnostic' teaching in the ancient world was far from uniform. The label conveniently describes a wide variety of heretical ideas about creation, salvation and behaviour. Wherever genuine truth is expounded the devil will always make sure that innocent seekers are provided with attractive but erroneous and ineffective substitutes. Gnostic teaching in its various forms came to be recognised by Christians as a counterfeit message.

The gnosticism which is opposed by New Testament writers is of differing varieties. In the first century this kind of false doctrine was still being shaped and formulated; by the late second century, a Christian theologian, Irenaeus, could identify an astonishing array of different forms in his extensive study, *Against Heresies*. Traces of these ideas in their early stages were clearly troubling the churches by the time 1 John and the Pastoral epistles were written and it is likely that it was teaching of this kind which Paul sought to counteract in Colossians. Some gnostic teachers incorporated Christian elements in their teaching; others clearly did not. It is possible that Timothy and Paul had encountered a distinctively Jewish form of this heresy, and that some aspects of the Pastoral epistles are designed to combat this.

Writing at the turn of the second and third centuries a gifted Christian teacher, Clement of Alexandria, said that the gnostics were passionately devoted to an exploration of these themes: ' . . . who we were and what we have become, where we were, where we were placed, whither we hasten, from what we are redeemed, what birth is, what re-birth?' The subjects they mentioned could hardly be of greater importance, but Christian preachers affirmed that the honest quest for these aspects of truth would never be satisfied by the pursuit of innumerable novel speculations but only by the study of God's revelation in Scripture and in the person of his Son, the unique Saviour of mankind.

For a more detailed study of the many facets of gnosticism see the IVP *Illustrated Bible Dictionary*, Vol. I, pp. 564–68.

Analysis of 1 Timothy

1:1–11 Keeping a straight course

Paul begins this letter to his young friend with a greeting which must have greatly cheered its first reader. Life was not easy for Timothy; naturally reticent, he had to cope also with 'frequent ailments' (5:23) and some doctrinally indifferent church members (3,4). Two reassuring truths are communicated to him in Paul's opening words: God's sovereignty and Christ's return. When God calls us to his work it is by his 'command' (1) and not our choice, and the believer's 'hope' is in Christ alone. From time to time Christian workers may be disappointed by lack of visible results and overwhelmed by a sense of failure or inadequacy, but they must recall that God has called them in the past and Christ will meet them in the future. The Lord's return is a powerful and persuasive incentive; when we meet him we will want to be known as his *faithful* servants (Matt. 25:23) who have kept their gaze on something more valuable than success or popularity. To have 'hope' in Christ is to have security, confidence and peace. Timothy must have been further encouraged to know that the apostle had confidence in him as a Christian worker. He had not only led him to personal faith in Christ ('child', 1 Cor. 4:17), but also regarded him as an outstanding colleague. As far as Paul was concerned, there was 'no one like him' (Phil. 2:20–22). Do people put that kind of value on our Christian partnership and service?

Timothy needed all the encouragement he could get, for it was hard to minister for Christ in first–century Ephesus. Some of the believers there had quickly forgotten what the apostle had written to them and others about acting like spiritual infants (Eph. 4:14). Cunning men with highly speculative (4) and spiritually dangerous (19) teaching had created troubles in the church; their message owed more to human ingenuity than divine inspiration (4:7; 2 Tim. 3:16). Such fanciful notions did not lead to godliness and higher moral standards. 'Sound doctrine' (10) can be tested by examining both its effects (4, 5, compare 6:3–5) and source. Dismissing unprofitable teaching, Paul rejoices in the astounding news of God's redemptive glory in Christ (11). 'The law is an excellent thing' (NEB) because it exposes sin (8–10); these damaging teachers had probably allegorised, explained away, or rejected the law. Alan Stibbs has reminded us that the law 'supports and complements the gospel by forbidding everything that is opposed to its wholesome teaching'.

THOUGHT: To be 'entrusted' with 'the gospel which tells of the glory of God' (11, NEB) is a spiritually exacting responsibility as well as a totally undeserved privilege. Such treasure is to be shared not hidden, proclaimed not obscured.

1:12–17 Even me!

Paul is overwhelmed when he considers it is not *in spite of* his former antagonism and opposition that he has been 'entrusted' (11) with the gospel, but that it may be *because of* his earlier rejection of Christ that the 'blessed God' not only saved him (15), but commissioned him as an apostle (1,12). He would for ever be a lasting example of God's grace lavished (14, NEB) on a particularly fierce, unattractive blasphemer, and of Christ's patience with one who had abused and insulted him (13, compare the behaviour of some other opponents of Christ, Matt. 26:67; 27:26–31, 39–44). If the opening verses of the letter (1–11) emphasise the importance of wholesome teaching, this passage inspires us with the necessity of uninhibited evangelism.

Four things are worthy of special note, particularly by those who seek to win others for Christ in this generation: (*a*) Paul is grateful that in his weakness (2 Cor. 12:7–10), hardship (2 Cor. 11:23–28) and difficulties (2 Cor. 11:12–15; Phil. 1:15) he has been *'given . . . strength'* (12). This generously bestowed energy (Phil. 4:13) made him 'equal to the task' (12, NEB); without it he would have abandoned the fight, collapsed in the race, or forsaken the cause (compare 2 Tim. 4:7) as others had certainly done (19,20; 2 Tim. 4:10,16). That same strength was not only available to Timothy (2 Tim. 2:1); it is ours too (Acts 1:8). (*b*) Paul was *'judged . . . faithful'*. In this matter the Lord's omniscient wisdom was manifest, as well as his omnipotent power. The Lord knew he would be dependable and 'worthy of this trust' (NEB). It is more than an astonishing compliment; it is a further testimony to the biblical assurance that whenever God calls a man or woman to service he equips them with everything good (Heb. 13:20,21). (*c*) Paul had *'received mercy'*. Twice in this passage (13,16) he refers to the Lord's undeserved dealings with him as an ignorant (13) rebel. Forsyth complained that some believers have 'nothing apostolic or missionary' in their service; 'they have never known the soul's despair or its breathless gratitude.' (*d*) Paul *shared truth* (15). The sure sayings of the gospel are 'words you may trust' (15, NEB).

THOUGHT: After Paul's unforgettable encounter with the living Christ (Acts 9:1–9), nobody would ever be able to say that he or she was too bad to be a believer or that God's merciful grace could not possibly reach as far as a blaspheming, persecuting, truth-rejecting opponent.

1:18–2:7 Prayer and love

As surely as Paul's apostolic ministry was by divine appointment, so was Timothy's. After all, the inspired utterances of trusted Christians (18) had pointed him out as a man entirely suitable for service (compare Acts 13:1–3 where the Holy Spirit gave similar instructions to the believers at Antioch through their leaders). Assurance of the divine initiative combined with the spiritual confidence and supportive fellowship of other Christians ought to encourage Timothy to press on with the work and its warfare. He was in the powerful hands of the omnipotent God (17), but those who had caused havoc in the lives of others (19,20) had been 'delivered to Satan', excommunicated from the local church (the community where 'the king of ages' is honoured) to the world, the sphere where the devil's desires and objectives are constantly pursued. The church of Christ must be a praying (2:1,2) and a welcoming (2:3–7) community. The apostle believes that Christians have clear responsibilities in society and one (but not the only one) of them is that of intelligent intercession. First, they must pray for *all* men (note how that word recurs in the following verses) – those who have been severely disciplined by the church (20), as well as those who are greatly loved. Do we only pray for the people we like? Secondly, Timothy's congregations are to pray for kings, even for godless, aggressive emperors. Do we pray regularly for the great world leaders, or are we content to be disobedient to Scripture in this matter? Thirdly, Timothy's people are to pray for 'all in high office' (NEB), which includes ministers of state, local government officers, and anyone in an influential position in life. The prayer interests of many Christians rarely stray beyond the confines of the local church. Unlike the exclusive and insular gnostic sects, the local church must be a *welcoming* community. God desires the salvation of *all* and Christ gave himself as a ransom for *all* (4,6), not just for the initiated and favoured few, as the gnostic teachers insisted. The words do not support the idea of inevitable salvation for everyone, but they do insist on the universal *appeal* of the gospel which can reach even blasphemers (1:13), heretics (20) and apathetic rulers (1,2), if they will repent.

THOUGHT: The objective Word of God and the inward sentinel of sensitive human conscience are God's sanctifying instruments. They work together in our lives to produce holiness of life and spiritual integrity.

2:8–15 Adorning the gospel

Paul turns now from the exhortation to pray (1,2) to its prerequisites. Our 'supplications' (1) will be but empty words unless we approach God as he demands. The fractious, quarrelsome (8) person, out of harmony with his fellows, is not likely to be heard. This means we will not harbour resentments or foster ill-feeling of any kind. The Christ who, by his unique sacrifice, has won 'freedom for all mankind' (6, NEB) does not wish us to be controlled by jealous attitudes, moody or angry thoughts. The passage seems to suggest that all men had both the freedom and encouragment to pray at Christian meetings. It was not the exclusive prerogative of the minister or leader. Congregational participation in worship was of great spiritual importance in the life of the early churches (1 Cor. 12:4–11; 14:26–33). The uplifted hands outwardly express dependence on God (see Exod. 17:11,12; Ps. 63:4); the unresentful spirit indicates peace with men. Both are vital if prayer is to be heard and answered.

The selective reference to *men* at prayer causes Paul to turn to the spiritual responsibilities of *women*. It is hardly meant to imply that women are not ever permitted to pray publicly and audibly (see 1 Cor. 11:5). That the prayer responsibility should be assigned to men is natural in a first–century setting with the church's 'synagogue' background. The apostle does not approve of women teachers (12), though he was clearly indebted to women for sacrificial service in the churches (see Rom. 16:1–16). Paul suggests that, in first–century society, where godless women, by dress, jewellery, cosmetics and behaviour (9), blatantly drew attention to themselves, it was an appropriate testimony to the transforming grace of Christ if Christian women drew attention to the gospel (10) which had changed their values. Paul argues that the submissive spirit is more fitting in Christian women than the self-assertiveness shown by Eve (13,14). God's purpose is that the man should lead, but the woman's influential role in the home is beyond question. God will be good to her, preserving her in childbirth (15), and she will be a radiant example to her children, a loyal partner to her husband, helpful to her parents (5:16) and a hospitable friend to the needy (5:10).

REMEMBER: William Law reminds us that prayer can help us to love someone difficult: 'There is nothing that makes us love a man so much as praying for him . . . This will fill your heart with a generosity and tenderness that will give you a better and sweeter behaviour than anything that is called fine breeding or good manners.'

3:1–7 Qualifications for leadership

Paul comes now to the 'noble task' (1) of the ministry. The term 'office of bishop' (*episkopē*) means 'oversight' or 'leadership' (1, NEB) and the requirements listed here emphasise the importance of appropriate leaders in Christ's work. There are five realms in which the necessary qualifications can be tested. First, and most important of all, the personal factors are enumerated (2,3a). He must not only be 'above reproach' so that people cannot charge him with inconsistent behaviour; he must have attractive and exemplary qualities, being self-controlled, courteous and kind.

Secondly, his financial affairs should be in good order (3b). The church leader will be compelled at times to handle other people's money in the course of his church work, so he must not be a 'lover' of it, exposing himself and others to temptation. The New Testament has a good deal to say about the right attitude to money, especially on the part of Christian workers.

Thirdly, his family life must be a good example to others (4,5). The contented family unit was a unique testimony to Christ's power in the first century and later when domestic life was often sordid and depraved. We appear to have returned to these distressing features in the twentieth century where many marriages seem doomed to end in divorce. The situation is terribly sad, but it presents Christians with an opportunity to display the peace, love, loyalty and security of family life at its very best.

Fourthly, in the spiritual realm, the leader must be a capable teacher (2b) and a mature believer (6). He must have the ability to communicate the truth effectively to others, but he should not be a young convert, one who has had no opportunity to prove the truths to which he is sincerely committed. We do not help young Christians by compelling them to 'run' before they have had an opportunity to 'walk' with Christ.

Finally, the leader must have good social qualities. He needs to be 'hospitable' with his home (2) and 'have a good reputation with the non-Christian public' (7a, NEB) 'which is ready enough to oppose the Christian faith; there is no need to multiply its opportunities by unnecessary scandal' (Barrett). When the devil brings a Christian leader down (7b) he has caused considerable (in some cases irreparable) damage to Christ's cause. Do we pray enough for those who have accepted this 'noble task'?

A NECESSARY PLEA: 'Moreover, take heed to yourselves, lest your example contradict your doctrine . . . lest you may unsay with your lives which you say with your tongues . . . He that means as he speaks will surely do as he speaks' (Richard Baxter).

3:8–13 The best deacons

At this point Paul turns to the qualities required of deacons and their wives. There are a number of clear similarities; compare, for example, the attitudes to strong drink and money (2,8) and the importance of good family life (4,12). Deacons were the servants of the local congregations with primary responsibility for the practical needs of the people, especially the lonely, poor and sick. Read Acts 6:1–6 and note that although 'serving tables' was a mundane duty, it demanded people with spiritual qualities. Stephen and his colleagues had to be men of great wisdom, filled with the Spirit and well respected by the people. Paul emphasises Christian maturity as an essential prerequisite for this kind of service among the people of God. The deacon's conversation (8) is naturally important when his work demands the visitation of Christian homes, especially in times of adversity. His speech must not be inconsistent (a living lie), insincere (saying one thing in one house and the opposite in another), nor destructive (compare 'slanderers' in v. 11). Every believer needs to ask that he or she will not be guilty of becoming one of Bunyan's Mr. Two-Tongues. Leaders must not only have commendable conversation but spiritual confidence (9); faith's *mystery* genuinely held by these deacons is 'the open secret of God's truth hidden to man's unaided reason but revealed in Christ' (Ronald Ward). It is the deposit of God's truth, personally accepted, continually appreciated and conscientiously manifested in daily living, not just a set of doctrinal ideas which a man can 'churn out' to order. A 'clear conscience' is, in Kelly's words, 'free from stain and self-reproach'. Deacons must be those who have proved themselves to be genuine Christians and therefore approved by their fellow believers (10), of 'good standing' in the local church and in the sight of God (13). Verse 11 refers to the qualities necessary either for the deacon's wife or for the role of the deaconess. The spiritual effectiveness of many a leader's ministry has been more than doubled by the dedicated surrender and supportive partnership of a good wife; conversely, a man whose partner is flippant, garrulous, uncontrolled and disloyal (all four dangers are behind the description in v. 11) is likely to find his best work undone, hindered and minimised.

A WARNING: When husband and wife do not share the Christian faith they are thereby kept apart from each other in many of the most important issues of life. Spiritual estrangement is inevitable. Christians contemplating marriage have a special responsibility to give the most serious consideration to the teaching of 2 Corinthians 6:14–18.

3:14–4:5 The church and its message

Following his instruction about the church's intercessions (ch. 2) and leaders (ch. 3), Paul now deals with the church's nature (15), message (16) and opponents (4:1–5). The church is a family ('household') where love is dominant; it is the creation and possession of 'the living God' and he controls its destiny (see Matt. 16:18). Paul may even be making a deliberate contrast specially meaningful to believers at Ephesus where Timothy worked; the temple to Diana or Artemis was occupied by a dead idol, not a living God. That temple had 127 ornate marble pillars clearly visible to all. God's church openly witnesses to the truth; guarding the deposit as a 'bulwark' is not Timothy's task alone (6:20) but that of the whole church. Contrast also 'Great is Artemis of the Ephesians' (Acts 19:28,34) with 'Great is the mystery of *our* religion.' In this description (15,16) the church is a loving family, a living organism and a loyal witness.

The church's message is presented in verse form, probably a quotation from an early Christian hymn; it is all about the Christ who loved the church, gave himself up for it, and sanctified it, a truth familiar to the Ephesians (Eph. 5:25–27). The real humanity of Jesus ('manifested in the flesh') is important in view of the gnostic asceticism described as heresy in the following verses. But he was not simply a good man; the Holy Spirit vindicated ('shown to be right') Christ as God's unique Son. However, 'Spirit' may refer to Christ's Spirit (compare Rom. 1:4). 'Seen by angels' may be a resurrection or ascension reference, Christ being made known as the triumphant Lord to the principalities and powers (1 Pet. 3:22). This message of the exalted Christ ('taken up in glory') is universally to be 'preached' by the church and 'believed' by the whole world ('nations'). It is not for the specially favoured gnostic few.

But there are those who neither treasure it nor proclaim it. God's Spirit (4:1) not only reminds the church of Christ's teaching (John 14:26; 15:26; 16:13–15); he warns the church of Christ's enemies. These gnostic teachers maintained that all 'matter' is evil. Denying the work of a loving Creator (4), these heretics held that celibacy and dietary laws were preferable and superior to marriage and normal eating habits. We should give thanks that the God who made man and the material world, and his Son who became incarnate, have provided good things for our enjoyment (6:17).

A SUGGESTION: Make a note of the things in this day which ought to have been 'received with thanksgiving' (4). It is not too late to express gratitude to him.

Questions for further study and discussion on 1 Timothy 1:1–4:5

1. How does one reconcile what Paul says here (1:9,10), that the law is really for the lawless, with what he says in Romans, which infers that it is necessary for believers as well as unbelievers (see Rom. 3:19; 7:21, 22)?

2. In the light of what the apostle says in these chapters about 'conscience', especially 1:19; 4:2 (compare 1:5; 3:9), how reliable is one's conscience as a moral sentinel or guide in life? How can its intuitions be checked?

3. If 'thanksgivings' are to be made 'for all men' (2:1), who would appear on your list? Are such people mentioned regularly by you in prayer?

4. In times like ours, when alcoholism is as serious a threat as drugs, how should Christians react to the notes of caution and appeal to example in these verses about leadership responsibilities and (3:3,8; also 5:23) drinking? How does one relate total abstinence to the teaching of 4:4,5; 6:17b?

5. Look again at the extract from a first–century hymn in 3:16 and consider six elements which you would wish to include in such a hymn of confession of special relevance in the late twentieth century.

6. How should the qualifications for church leaders, outlined by Paul, be applied today?

7. What can we learn from the brief hints in the New Testament about the place of excommunication in church discipline (1:19,20; compare 1 Cor. 5:3–5)?

8. List some contemporary ideas about the nature of Jesus. How would you respond to them in the light of Paul's teaching?

4:6–11 Hope set on the living God

Paul's ambition is that Timothy will not simply be a minister, but 'a *good* minister of Christ Jesus' (6). These verses describe a really 'good' leader. First of all, he (or she) must exercise a teaching function (6, 11). Paul has passed 'these instructions' on to Timothy not simply for his own interest and guidance; they must be handed on to others and 'put . . . before the brethren' (6, compare 2 Tim. 2:2). Note how the emphasis on good teaching recurs throughout these letters (4:11,13,16; 6:2b–3; 2 Tim. 2:2,15,24; 4:2; Titus 2:1,15). Whatever the nature of our specific work for Christ, it ought to provide us with some opportunity to share verbally the truth of God's Word. Not all are preachers but all have something special to say.

Secondly, the leader must recognise a disciplinary obligation. If he is to declare the Word to others, he must continually (6a) receive it for himself. His life needs feeding regularly (present participle). The word is both the nourishment he receives and the truth he pursues (6b). It is not enough to read it; one must practise it too if one is to be an effective teacher of others and not a harmful hypocrite. This kind of discipline is essential training for the Christian athlete (7b–8; 1 Cor. 9: 25–27; 2 Tim. 2:5); it demands effort and persistence.

Thirdly, the leader must develop a discerning spirit (7a). Paul's message was not the only religious teaching which was going round the churches. Perpetrators of 'godless and silly myths' were creating havoc in the lives of some believers. Unbiblical notions are still proclaimed by an increasing number of sects in our own day. Christians need to be able to discern between what is true and edifying, and what is erroneous and harmful (1 Thess. 5:21,22; 1 John 4:1).

Fourthly, the leader needs an eternal perspective. He will bring his best to consistent witness and compassionate service in this 'present life', but he will do all this far more conscientiously if he remembers 'the life to come' (8b). Our recognition of the future aspects of our faith will not issue in escapism but realism, optimism and hope (10).

Fifthly, the leader is sustained by the confident assurances of Scripture (9). He can say to his contemporaries, 'Here are words you may trust' (9, NEB, compare 1:15).

Finally, the leader rejoices in the universal generosity of God (10). It is for 'all men', not the specially select, highly privileged initiates of the gnostic sects. God is every man's Saviour *potentially*. Not all will believe; some will be lost. In a special sense, therefore, he is *certainly* the Saviour of those who trust his saving work in Christ for them.

AN ORDER TO OBEY: 'Train yourself in godliness' (7).

4:12–16 Take heed to yourself

Paul continues to emphasise the importance of God's Word within the life of the believing community. Scripture must be read publicly (as in the Synagogue) and expounded carefully (13), a ministry which will demand concentrated attention and persistence (15). The apostle concentrates here not only on Timothy's public duties (13,14), but also on his private responsibilities. He is not simply to declare the message vocally; he is to expound it silently by the way he lives. His behaviour is to be as eloquent as his sermons. Life is not easy for Timothy. False teachers are fiercely proclaiming a different message and he is probably slightly nervous and reticent in the exercise of his ministry (there are frequent hints of his timidity and ill-health throughout the two letters, 5:23; 2 Tim. 1:4,7,8; 2:1,3). It is possible that he may have felt unnecessarily self-conscious about his age (12). The apostle urges him to put aside that kind of hesitancy and insecurity. Age is not specially important; maturity most certainly is. He is to be a good example (12) to others so that his gospel is evident in his life as well as in his words. Remember Richard Baxter's warning to ministers and preachers in his *Reformed Pastor*, that they take care not to undo with their lives what they say with their tongues, that what they say on one day a week is not contradicted by how they act on the other six. Notice the perfect balance of Scripture: consistent example and faithful exhortation are meant to go together (12,13). The gift of ministry has to be used, nurtured and cultivated; a man engaged in this work must devote his energies to the improvement of these abilities: 'devote yourself to them' (15; compare 2 Tim. 1:6). The proper care of one's own spiritual life (16a) is an essential aspect of outgoing service.

We are not likely to be used for the salvation of others (16b) if we deliberately refuse to work out our own salvation (Phil. 2:12,13) in daily living. The 'teaching' God has given is our greatest treasure; 'hold to that'.

THOUGHT: In the sixth century Gregory the Great observed that 'there are some who . . . hasten to teach what they have learned, not by practice, but by study, and belie in their conduct what they teach by words . . . with what presumption does he hasten to heal the afflicted while he carries a sore on his own face'. The Venerable Bede said of Cuthbert that 'like a good teacher, he taught others only what he first practised himself.'

5:1–8 Widows and their work

Paul now provides young Timothy with explicit help about the right way to handle different people in the local congregation. The same truth must be fearlessly and faithfully declared to all (God has no favourites) but, as a skilful pastor, the apostle knows that all people are not meant to be treated exactly alike. One approach, fitting for young people, is probably inappropriate for the elderly. Paul's wisdom as an effective counsellor becomes clearly evident as one studies these verses. Some Christian workers become so obsessed by what they *want* that they become oblivious to how people *feel*. Time and again in the New Testament leaders are warned against the perils of dictatorship (e.g. Rom. 12:16; 1 Pet. 5:3; compare Mark 10:42–45; John 13:4,5,12–17). Be as respectful to older people as you would be to your father (Exod. 20:12; Lev. 19:32; compare Lam. 5:12); similarly, be as grateful and compassionate to older women in the church as you would be to your own mother, recognising as you do that some are 'mothers in Israel' to younger believers. Heighten the family consciousness of the church by treating people of similar age to yourself as brothers and sisters.

Paul then turns to the right attitude to widows. God has a particular concern for them (Ps. 68:5; Deut. 10:18), and just as Israel cared for them (Exod. 22:22; Deut. 24:17) so must the church (Acts 6:1). Two aspects of their responsibility seem to emerge here. In the local church they must be officially recognised (3,9) and lovingly supported (4,8); a list (9) ensures that these needy people are not overlooked. Such women served as deaconesses, fulfilling spiritual and practical functions within the local congregation. It is good that the church's social concern is given prominence here. Widows must be cared for by their families; the elderly must be honoured and loved, and appropriate provision made for their welfare by their children and grandchildren (4). The right approach to Christian widowhood is enumerated in verses 5,6; the point being reinforced by a contrast between the devoted, trusting intercessor and the self-centred indulgent woman, only concerned for her own enjoyment. Those Christians who do not take their extended family responsibilities seriously are severely condemned and described in terms reminiscent of apostasy and godlessness.

THOUGHT: Timothy must admonish an older man as he would a father. Hendricksen says: 'How considerately, with what tact, what gentleness and moderation, would he deal with one who stood so close to him! Let him then treat this erring one with the same humility, love and tenderness. For, after all, the Christian community is a family, the most glorious family of all (Matt. 12:49,50).'

5:9–16 Godly work for women

The apostle now turns to consider the official list of carefully selected and financially supported widows (or deaconesses) kept by these local churches with whom he and Timothy are familiar. The qualifications necessary for this form of early Christian social service are enumerated in today's passage. Throughout Paul's teaching on this subject there is the clear distinction between what the family must do (care for its elderly people) and what the church ought to do (look after those who have no one else who cares for them). The church must not usurp the family's responsibility in this matter, nor must Christians imagine that their fellow believers will shoulder a spiritual duty which is plainly their own (16; compare 8). Paul distinguishes clearly between younger and older widows, believing that the younger widow may well re-marry (14) and, with that perfectly natural prospect on her heart, is not normally suited to the work he has in mind. Some very unhappy experience of the unsuitability of the younger widow for this ministry doubtless lies behind the strong sayings in verses 11–15.

Given this sole reservation and age restriction about the ministry of widows, Paul is certain that suitable women have a most important function to fulfil within the life of the spiritually active and socially aware congregation. Their Christian experience prior to widowhood is regarded as the finest qualification for future service. They will be people who have cared naturally for others even when things were well with themselves. When that experience is considered one can easily see how dedicated godly women could fulfil a highly important role in contemporary church life as well as in the first century, for example, pastoral visitation, the care of orphans, the provision of hospitality for the church's guests, ministry to the sick; all of these emerge naturally from the pre-widowhood features described in verse 10. Whilst ministry of this kind could be of incalculable benefit to Christians and unbelievers in a local community, consider (as Paul does, v. 13) the havoc which could be done by unsuitable people engaged in the visitation of homes. We do well to remember that what we do for Christ in service is not nearly so important as the way we do it. Work poorly done is more of a victory for Satan (14,15) than a sacrifice for Christ.

PRAYER: 'Lord, make me an instrument of your peace, a means of grace and a channel of blessing to others in this day.'

5:17–25 Practical counsel

At this stage in the letter the apostle provides help for Timothy about the place of elders in the local church. Paul is specially concerned about their financial support (17,18) and their exposure to criticism (19,20). Excellent work should be recognised by worthy remuneration ('double stipend', 17, NEB), particularly in the case of preachers and teachers. But Paul's commitment to this is based not on human generosity but on biblical convictions (18). Note how, for the apostle, Old Testament teaching (Deut. 25:4; compare 1 Cor. 9: 9–11,14) is placed alongside the sayings of Jesus (Luke 10:7; Matt. 10:10) as 'Scripture', God's uniquely inspired Word, always profitable for our instruction (2 Tim. 3:16) and intensely practical even about down-to-earth issues like a man's wages. Timothy and his colleagues must make sure that, if accusations are made against an elder's conduct (19), reports are checked (compare Deut. 19:15; Matt. 18:16) and confirmed by reliable people; good workers have sometimes been destroyed by malicious gossip. Those who 'persist in sin' (20) may refer either to the unscrupulous accusers or the guilty elder; in either case public rebuke is a warning to others. The exercise of discipline is never easy, but one must guard against favouritism (21). The leadership of a local church is far too serious a matter to be entrusted to unsuitable or immature people (22). Some have suggested that the 'laying on of hands' here refers to a practice (known to exist in the third century) whereby penitents were publicly readmitted to the church in this way, but there is no evidence for this in the first century and ordination is doubtless intended here. To act irresponsibly by participating in the ordination of an unsuitable person is to identify with the offender's sins, though the responsibility to decide or judge on such matters demands sincerity and moral purity on Timothy's part (22b). At first, verse 23 appears to be a strange intrusion, but Kelly suggests that it follows naturally after 'keep yourself pure' or unstained. Drunkenness was a serious danger (see 3:3,8; Tit. 1:7). Leon Morris reminds us that in our society, 'when the causes of sickness are better known, it is possible to get the required result without resorting to the use of wine'. Fear of its effects may have discouraged Timothy from its use in any circumstances and Paul is here saying that medically it could be helpful. Everything in our lives is exposed to God's scrutiny. Secret or otherwise (24), good deeds also ultimately become known to men (25). How important it is therefore to have a 'clear conscience' (3:9; 2 Tim. 1:3).

A COMMAND: 'Keep yourself pure' (22).

6:1,2 Unqualified respect

Paul has been reminding Timothy that all our conduct ultimately becomes conspicuous, good and bad alike (5:25); this truth leads naturally to a consideration of the Christian's employment, particularly with reference to those believers at Ephesus and elsewhere who were slaves. There were vast numbers of slaves throughout the Roman world – 60 million is one estimate. Understandably, in the light of these huge numbers, they were feared, 'kept under' and sometimes brutally treated. The presence of slaves in the churches (compare, e.g. Eph. 6:5–9; Tit. 2:9; Philm. 16) naturally posed problems for Christian leaders. At his work and/or in the home the slave was socially inferior, but in the church he was spiritually equal (Gal. 3:28), a brother or sister of his fellow members. Brash or thoughtless slaves might presume on the goodwill of their Christian masters; some guidance ought to be offered to them. The issues raised here are not of merely antiquarian interest. There are some guiding principles which may well be helpful in our twentieth-century attitude to work, a topic of crucial importance in contemporary society. The first point made here is that the employer must be respected (1a). Some concept of authority and leadership (responsibly maintained) is essential in any well-ordered community. Without it, one is exposed to anarchy. The Christian slave must 'honour' his master and not simply do his work ungrudgingly. Furthermore, good work must be recognised as a highly effective form of Christian witness (1b). Honouring God by honest and commendable employment is even more important than honouring the master. God's name is likely to be dishonoured and his truth bitingly criticised if the conduct of a Christian at work is lazy, insolent or half-hearted. People are not likely to accept what we say if we are idle, dishonest, or produce poorer work than our unbelieving colleagues. Good slaves will 'adorn the doctrine' (Tit. 2:9,10), not dishonour it. Paul goes on to emphasise that the Christian master or employer has every right to expect *more* of a believing slave or employee simply because he is a fellow Christian (2a). These employees are 'slaves of Christ' (Eph. 6:6, RSV margin) and belong to him (1 Cor. 6:19,20) who expects us to work devotedly (Col. 3:22), honestly (Tit. 3:1) and expectantly (Col. 3:24). Truths such as these must form part of Timothy's regular teaching (2b).

THOUGHT: In our daily occupation we must remember that the believer's work, and all else in his life, is for *Christ*, not simply for the boss.

6:3–10 Don't love money

After dealing with the issue of slaves and their masters, Paul goes on to consider other people in or around the local church, wrangling controversialists (3–5), ambitious materialists (9,10, 17–19) and, by contrast, young Timothy himself (11–16, 20,21). There is a strangely modern ring about the message of these verses. The false teaching which Paul here condemns tells us more about the self-seeking motives of the teachers than the ideas they are trying to convey. They traffic in these godless notions (contrast v. 3b) in order to parade themselves and their conceit (4). The 'pompous ignoramus' (4, NEB) of this kind promotes his so-called 'knowledge' (4b, 5a; compare 1:4; 4:7; Tit. 3:9) as a gnostic teacher with his bizarre speculations and metaphysical fancies, all in the hope of making a pile of money (5b) out of unsuspecting customers. Teachers of this kind were not only reprehensible because of the profit motive, but because they had spawned their deceptive ideas out of diseased minds. Such depraved teaching was absolutely opposed to the 'wholesome' health-giving message contained in the gospel (3, NEB).

The mention of financial gain by these gnostic propagandists leads Paul to issue Timothy with a warning about money and its dangers. In itself, there is nothing wrong with money at all; indeed, it can be used to bring help to the needy (18) and proper enjoyment for ourselves (17). But to love it so much that, whatever happens, its quantity must be increased is to be trapped in a deadly snare, oppressed by a self-wounding passion, plunged into a pit of destructive ruin; all these sobering images are heaped up in verses 9,10. It is a craving which can never be satisfied, causing some deliberately to turn from the way of faith to a course of ultimate rejection. Possessions cannot be transferred to eternity (7). There are 700 million people in our world who each exist on less than 10p a day; if we have more than adequate food and clothing (8), surely God has been more than generous to us. It is wrong to complain when we have so much. The prison-testimony of Philippians 4:11 has become a persuasive truth in verse 8. How deeply do you share Paul's conviction about a simple life–style? Godly contentment is the richest of all blessings; to be utterly satisfied with him and all he graciously gives is to be happy indeed.

MEDITATE on the song of the shepherd boy in Bunyan's *Pilgrim's Progress* (Part Two):

> I am content with what I have,
> Little be it, or much;
> And, Lord, contentment still I crave,
> Because thou savest such.

6:11–21 Rich in faith

The 'man of God' (11) must deliberately shun both false teaching (3–5) and false seeking (9,10), but Paul knows that a man cannot survive spiritually on negatives. He must pursue rich, positive qualities and virtues, making his daily ambition these, rather than the applause of an admiring crowd fascinated by his novel teaching or the increase of his financial assets. The Christian worker will not find it easy; we are engaged in a battle (12) and conquests will only be made by steadfast heroes resolutely determined to please their commander. To become 'entangled' by the lust either for popularity or possessions is to disappoint the one who enlisted us (2 Tim. 2:3,4). The summons to courageous action (12) and bold confession causes Paul to reflect on the most memorable testimony of all time, that of Christ as he fought the sinister powers of evil (John 12:31; Col. 2:14,15; Heb. 2:14,15), especially during the closing hours of his earthly life (13). He spoke boldly before Pilate, though he knew only too well where it would lead him. Timothy must not only recall Christ's passion but also his promised return (14,15). As in 1:12–17, the 'testimony' ends with a doxology (15,16), a chorus of exaltation magnifying the name of a God who is sovereign (15), living, holy (16), as well as generous (17). Unlike verses 9, 10, verses 17–19 appear to be addressed to wealthy Christians who come within Timothy's pastoral responsibility. Their most valuable possession is the 'eternal life' (12b,19) they possess both here and now, not perishable assets. Their money must be put to good use, but they must be more than lavish benefactors. Like the poorest members, the wealthy must also be generous in 'good deeds', activities which demand meaningful identification, sensitive concern, a compassionate visit – the use of time, not just money. Important and helpful as it is, writing a cheque is no substitute for personal involvement. Love is worth more than a pound-note. Timothy must warn the rich members about pride (17), remind them of eternity (19) and, for his part, he must continue to be a faithful guardian (20) of the world's greatest treasure, the imperishable gospel.

CHALLENGE: In this closing passage Paul can turn confidently from false teachers and money-makers to reliable Timothy, 'But . . . you' (11) is emphatic (see 2 Tim. 2:1; 3:10,14; 4:5 for similar reference to this contrast). Can our ministers or church leaders say the same about us?

Questions for further study and discussion on 1 Timothy 4:6–6:21

1. Those universalists who assert that in the end all men, believers and unbelievers alike, will be saved use 2:4; 4:10 and 2 Pet. 3:9 as biblical support for their teaching. How would you expound these verses in the light of other New Testament teaching about judgement?

2. Outline a job-description for a Christian widow or deaconess employed and supported by your local church. In what way could a woman of the kind mentioned by Paul (5:10) bring spiritual help and social service to a church and enhance its witness in the local community?

3. How does one distinguish between those Old Testament injunctions which are to be obeyed (5:18,19) and those now superseded by Christ, his work and teachings?

4. Why is the exercise of discipline generally neglected by the local church (5:20) until the sin is so serious that some action cannot be avoided? What place should be given to compassionate correction before our 'errors' develop into 'presumptuous sins' or the 'great transgression' (Ps. 19:12,13)?

5. Re-read 6:6–10, 17–19 and consider by what practical means a Christian can ensure that his life is not gradually squeezed into the world's mould (see Rom. 12:2, especially J. B. Phillips' paraphrase) of contemporary materialism.

6. Suggest a programme of 'training' (see 4:7,8 and comment) for a new Christian. How might it differ for, say, a teenager at college, a factory worker, a busy housewife and mother?

7. Discuss the basis on which your church pays its 'full time' workers, in the light of 5:17,18 and related passages.

8. Timothy's life and service were clearly marked by outstanding ability. In another letter Paul said that, in the course of their work together, his younger colleague had 'proved his worth' (Phil. 2:22, TEV). Which would you consider to be Timothy's most attractive qualities for the ministry?

Analysis of 2 Timothy

1:1–5 Thanking God

This short letter, probably the last of Paul's extant writings (4:6–8) is designed to encourage and instruct his spiritual son (2) in his difficult work. Troubled by emotional stress (4), physical weakness (1 Tim. 5:23) and, possibly, a nervous temperament (7,8), and certainly oppressed by quarrelsome opponents (2:23–26) and counterfeit teachers (3:8,9), Timothy needs this apostolic exhortation. Paul has the authority to say such things to his young colleague; he is God's 'apostle' (Luke 6:13; Acts 26:16–18) whatever others may say (1 Cor. 9:1,2; 2 Cor. 12:11–13). Here, as elsewhere at the beginning of his letters, Paul declares his divine appointment and message. It is by God's sovereign 'will' (1a) that he serves in this important ministry; his message is that of God's saving promise (1b), the gift of new, abundant and eternal life in Christ (2 Cor. 5:17; John 10:10; John 3:36; 5:24; 1 John 5:12).

Our writer is supremely grateful not only that he is engaged in worthwhile work and entrusted with the gospel of life (1), but for other things as well. Thanksgiving (3) is the dominant note of this opening section, even though the writer is in prison, facing death. Paul is thankful for the opportunity of continuing service, the joy of worship 'with a pure intention' (NEB), for his rich spiritual heritage in the Old Testament, for good parental influence (in his own life and Timothy's), for the privilege of prayer (all suggested by verse 3), for a loyal and loving colleague, for the joy of Christian fellowship (4), for proof of his effective ministry in a genuine convert who has a deep personal faith and is going on to maturity (5). Does 'thanksgiving' (Phil. 4:6; Rom. 1:21, 'did not . . . give thanks') play any appreciable part in our daily devotional life? Paul is not content simply to exhort others to thanksgiving (1 Tim. 2:1); he practises it himself. 'I serve . . . as did my fathers' (3); both the writer and recipient of this letter are grateful that in early life they had become 'acquainted with the sacred writings' (3:15). A passage such as this reminds us of the Christian parent's important role in the home as a privileged teacher as well as a good example. Timothy's unbelieving father was Greek, his mother a Jewess (Acts 16:1); now grandmother, mother and son have all received 'the promise of life which is in Christ Jesus' (1). What are we handing on to our children, neighbours, friends? The gospel is the most valuable heirloom in the world.

THOUGHT: John Newton wrote of his mother's influence: 'When I was four years old I could read with propriety in any common book. She stored my memory, which was then very retentive, with many valuable pieces, chapters, and portions of Scripture, catechisms, hymns and poems.'

1:6–14 Away with fear!

In addition to what was handed on to Timothy by his mother, grand-mother and Paul, he has also received a distinctive gift (*charisma*) directly from God at the beginning of his ministry (6). But, although initially imparted, it has constantly to be developed and responsibly exercised. Timothy must re-kindle the gift and keep it 'in full flame'. With his rich heritage (3–5), personal gift (6) and encouraging colleagues (4), there is no room for shrinking cowardice (8) or lack of confidence. He who supplies the resources overcomes the obstacles. The 'spirit of timidity' (7), although understandable, is unwarranted when we have the powerful (Acts 1:8), loving (Rom. 5:5) Holy Spirit who empowers us, produces love within us (Gal. 5:22) and makes us self-controlled (Gal. 5:23). Those who participate in Christ's work are certain to experience his sufferings (8). He said that would happen (Matt. 10:22; 24:9; John 15:18–21) and it did (1 John 3:13). But it is a privilege to share (Phil. 3:10), not an agony to avoid. We experience its pressures not in our own strength but 'in the power of God' (8). That strength is just as much God's gift to us as the gift of ministry (6) and the gift of salvation (9). The believer's 'holy calling' (9) is not simply to privilege but to identification with the Christ who endured suffering and abolished death (10). If Jesus has robbed death of its tyrannising power (Heb. 2:14,15), why be afraid of it? Like the living God (1 Tim. 3:15; 4:10; 6:16), the living Christ (2 Tim. 2:8) and the life-giving Spirit (2 Cor. 3:6), believers will live for ever. Although a prisoner and potential martyr, Paul is certainly 'not ashamed' (12). His radiant confidence is in the Christ who is well able to care for both the gospel he has entrusted to Paul (1 Tim. 1:11) *and* the life of the prisoner which has been entrusted to Christ (12, RSV margin). Paul rejoices in 'the faith and love which are in Christ Jesus' (13; compare 1 Tim. 1:14). These were not just key theological terms for Paul. God's gift of faith (Eph. 2:8) had banished his earlier unbelief, and love had supplanted his former hostility. These transforming truths had been committed to Timothy (14) as well as Paul (11). In a day like ours when many are only too eager to minimise or compromise, ridicule or ignore them, we must 'guard' the gospel and, like Timothy, we can do so in the power of the indwelling Spirit.

THOUGHT: Paul believes himself to be Christ's prisoner (8), not Caesar's prisoner. Every single aspect of his daily life is under the sovereign control of Christ, his conqueror (10) and guardian (12).

1:15–2:7 Persuasive portraits

For Paul, entering into the sufferings of Christ was not a vague, myst-ical experience. It meant, amongst other things, being prepared to face isolation and loneliness (15; 4:16; compare Matt. 26:56; John 16:32) for the gospel. Thank God that, even in the worst circumstances, there is usually some loyal believer around who will offer support and en-couragement (16,17). The man who offered public service in the church at Ephesus (18) was just as zealous about the largely unnoticed per-sonal ministry to one deserted believer in a Roman jail. Some long only for the limelight, but over the centuries most have been happy simply to serve. Onesiphorus was not ashamed (16) and Timothy must not be either (8). Paul earned the right to talk about suffering; he had experienced incredibly painful hardship and adversity (2 Cor. 11:24–29), but proved that with the awareness of weakness came the suffi-ciency of strength (2 Cor. 12:9,10 where, as here, in 2:1, 'grace' is strength). The gospel entrusted to Timothy (1:5; 2:2) must be handed on to those who will, in turn, pass it on to others. We are now at the late twentieth–century receiving end of this long line of faithful stew-ards; thank God for the millions who have not only received and treasured the good news, but passed it on to their contemporaries and successors.

Paul now draws a group of fascinating word pictures to impress upon Timothy's mind the importance of his work. The soldier, athlete and farmer (3–7) are followed later by the unashamed workman (15), the useful vessel (20,21) and the commendable servant (24,25). The soldier is an example of resolute endurance (3) and single-mindedness (4); he entertains no greater ambition than that of bringing pleasure to his commander. A model of submissive obedience, the athlete respects the rules; his skills must be kept within certain prescribed limits. He is not free to do whatever he pleases whilst he is running the race. There are rules and laws for Christ's followers; those who refuse to obey them (3:2–9; compare 1 Tim. 1:19,20) become aimless wanderers (1 Tim. 6:10; 2 Tim. 4:4) and helpless captives (2 Tim. 2:26) rather than the 'free' people they imagine themselves to be. The farmer illustrates strenuous activity; he knows that little will be achieved without effort. These portraits are to be kept constantly in view (7), for it is all too easy to become thoughtlessly entangled (4), carelessly disobedient (5) or just lazy (6). Remember that if we share the sufferings we shall share the strength (2:1) as well.

THOUGHT: The Lord enables his people to understand the truth (7) and provides them with the power to put it into practice.

2:8–19 The faithful workman

The rigorous demands of verses 3–6 may be overwhelming, but Timothy is urged to remember Jesus *risen* from the dead – perfect tense, meaning that this is not just a historical fact but a present reality, i.e. he is *now* risen, is wonderfully alive and always will be (Rom. 6:9). You do not have to work as a soldier, athlete and farmer in your own unaided energy. The fettered prisoner (9) glories in the unfettered truth of the Lord's messiahship ('Christ'), his unique deity and victorious conquest ('risen', compare Rom. 1:4), his perfect humanity and the fulfilment of Scripture in him ('descended from David', compare Rom. 1:3), his saving work (10), his reliable promise (11) and his coming reign (12). It is possible that, as in 1 Tim. 3:16 (and even 2 Tim. 1:9,10) we have further extracts here (11–13) from an early Christian hymn or confession of faith. Believers live in Christ now (2 Cor. 4:11; Rom. 6:5) and will live with him at death and always. Endurance (12) is always (present tense) expected of *all* believers, not just the valiant few like the apostle. He is prepared to endure for the sake of other believers (10); do our fellow believers mean as much to us? The 'denial' saying (12b) recalls the stern words of Jesus (Matt. 10:32,33) and is set alongside faithlessness (13) as a dreadful possibility. The truth that 'he remains faithful' does not contradict 'he also will deny us'; it confirms it. In John Stott's words, 'his "faithfulness" when we are faithless will be faithfulness to his warnings.' He does not act capriciously, declaring something one day and denying it the next (13b). He will act upon his warnings as well as his promises. The workman whose service for God is approved by him is one who faithfully conveys these truths, stern warnings as well as comforting promises, and does not handle Scripture selectively, ignoring those parts which are either unattractive to him or unacceptable to his contemporaries. The verb translated 'rightly handling' (15) is found elsewhere describing a ploughman driving a straight furrow, or someone 'cutting' a path or a road in a straight direction. It is used twice in the Greek version of the Old Testament (the Septuagint) at Prov. 3:6; 11:5. Instead of bringing faithful and helpful exposition to the people, some bring ruinous and infectious words ('spread like a gangrene', 17, NEB) with disastrous moral as well as spiritual consequences (14,16,18).

REMEMBER: Those who remain true to the faith both *stand* on the secure foundation of his reliable promise (19a) and *run* away from all that would defile them (19b).

2:20–26 Ready for any good work

In his first letter to Timothy Paul described the church as a house (3:15), but it is not necessary to insist that 'house' here (20) must be interpreted in precisely the same way. It *may* be a reference to the visible church with worthy and unworthy leaders ('vessels' as in 2 Cor. 4:7, the same word as that used here), but the illustration becomes forced if interpreted rigidly. Paul is more likely to be using this graphic imagery to illustrate and support what he has already said about the importance of avoiding contact with, and separating from, dangerous and unsound teachers (e.g. 14,16 and especially 19b). One is not meant to press the imagery, insisting that every item in the story symbolises some precise spiritual reality. It is more like a parable which invites us to search for the main point and not force every single detail into service. The main truth clearly presented by this vivid word picture is that the dedicated Christian is *inwardly pure, useful in service* and always *available to Christ*, all to be found in verse 21. 'So shun youthful passions' (22) continues and sustains the highly important 'personal purity' theme, but the verse goes on to emphasise the equally vital complementary truths – the pursuit of positive holiness as well as negative separation, and the recognition of corporate help ('along with those who call . . .') as well as individual responsibility. The gnostic controversialists had a disruptive and divisive effect among the first-century Christians (23); it is the very opposite to the 'peace' we are meant to possess and treasure (22; compare Gal. 5:22; Heb. 12:14a; 1 Pet. 3:8–11). The Lord's servant (or, literally, 'slave') must not be contentious as the heretics certainly are (23b,24); he has personal ('not quarrelsome'), pastoral ('kindly to everyone . . . forbearing'), didactic ('an apt teacher') and disciplinary ('correcting . . . with gentleness') responsibilities. Those who have forsaken God's unique message in Christ, preferring their own ideas to revealed truth, are in the devil's trap; he is delighted when they despise God's Word. The stark realism here is tempered by hope: even the worst of them can repent, accept the truth (25), and be released to do God's will (see RSV margin), not the enemy's. With Luther, we need to be 'captive to the Word'. Only thus can we escape the devil's subtle snare.

THOUGHT: 'Under the guise of prophetic righteousness, pride can move awakened believers to censorious attacks on other Christians, a lack of meekness in rebuking those who really need it . . . It can do things to Christians which make their religion grate painfully on the sensibilities of fellow-believers' (Richard Lovelace). By contrast, the Lord's servant 'is gentle as he corrects his opponents' (24, GNB).

3:1–9 Times of stress

Although the apostle begins this section of the letter by referring to false and immoral teachers who will be specially active in the 'last days' (1; compare 4:1–3), he has also encountered most of these nineteen evils amongst his own contemporaries, for he urges Timothy to avoid such people (5b). It is a sad catalogue of human sinfulness with its searing effect in the life of communities. That is possibly one of the most terrible things about sin – its power to reproduce itself in the lives of those who are sinned against. Families suffer (2, 'disobedient to their parents'), an essential care for others is absent (3, 'inhuman'), good people are tortured by cruel, untruthful accusations which are made against them (3, 'slanderers', literally 'devils', *diaboloi*), the innocent are corrupted by 'profligates'; it is not simply that such 'lovers of self' do nothing for others; they cannot bear those who do ('haters of good'). These people do not love God (4) and, although outwardly religious, know nothing of God's power to make them different (5). Such 'treacherous' people (4, Luke uses the word to describe Judas, 6:16) take advantage of the deep spiritual needs of the lonely, 'burdened with sins' (6); they are assured of a hearing in some homes where discernment is lacking and where any religious novelty is welcome (7). Remember that in the world of antiquity women were largely confined to their homes. Sheer boredom may have prepared the way for unhelpful visitors of this kind. Paul says that these corrupt teachers remind him of the Jannes and Jambres story (8) with which Timothy and others with an informed Jewish background were thoroughly familiar. Although not mentioned by name in the Old Testament, these two Egyptian magicians (Exod. 7:8–12; 9:11) appear in Jewish (e.g. the Damascus Document from Qumran), pagan and early Christian literature. Their opposition of Moses did not get them very far; 'counterfeit' first-century teachers (and their successors) will end up in the same way, for 'imposture is always tracked down in the end' (Guthrie). Those women who were so overwhelmed with guilt that they would 'listen to anybody' (6,7) did not find the help they needed because they lacked a genuine passion for 'the truth'. Many seeking people in our times wrongly pursue spiritual experience through the sects, occult and eastern mysticism. Sadly, they too 'will not get very far' (9).

THOUGHT: Remember the exclusive claim of Christ, 'I am the way, and the truth, and the life; no one comes to the Father, but by me' (John 14:6). This 'truth' has been proved in the experience of millions who, accepting his uniqueness, have been led to the Father.

Questions for further study and discussion on 2 Timothy 1:1–3:9

1. 2 Tim. 1:6 and 1 Tim. 4:14 have been used to support the idea that grace is mediated to us through appropriate individuals. If the idea does not appeal to you, what exactly did Paul mean by saying that Timothy's gift came 'through' (or 'with' as Barrett maintains) the laying on of the apostle's hands? What does this say about our own 'ordination' procedures?

2. What are the rules which determine the conduct of the Christian 'athlete' (2:5)? Is Paul hinting here at something more than moral conformity, e.g. 1 Cor. 3:5–15 with its suggestion that there are rules for Christian *work* as well as Christian *life*?

3. How does one answer the Christian who occasionally argues that since the coming of Christ there is no place for rules (2:5) or law in the life of a believer?

4. The resurrection (2:18) was clearly a stumbling-block to many listeners in the first century (Acts 17:18b, 31, 32; 24:15, 21) as it is to some of our contemporaries. Why is it such an integral and essential part of the Christian gospel (1 Cor. 15:12–19)?

5. What advice would you give to a Christian who is fearful? How should churches help such people?

6. Lonely women who spend all day bored at home are still a problem, especially on large housing estates. They easily fall prey to modern cults, sects and heresies. Suggest a practical programme for your church or group to bring such people Christian love and the 'promise of life'.

7. What do you think is involved in 'rightly handling the word of truth'? How might it be wrongly handled?

8. What can we learn from Paul's repeated injunctions to avoid pointless arguments (1 Tim. 1:4; 4:7; 6:20; 2 Tim. 2:14, 16, 23; compare 1 Tim. 6:5)?

3:10–13 As for you . . .

The words 'Now you' (10, compare 14: 'But as for you'), which begins this paragraph, contrast Timothy with these false and destructive teachers Paul has been mentioning (1–8) and to whom he returns (13). Timothy is completely different and Paul is grateful for that. He has 'words you may trust' (2:11, NEB). Instead of being influenced by charlatans and imposters, Timothy has followed Paul's teaching 'step by step' (10, NEB). He has not simply reproduced the apostle's message faithfully (commendable enough), but he has also paid particular attention to the way Paul ordered his personal life (10) and conducted his public ministry (11). With a natural hesitancy about drawing attention to ourselves, we may be a little puzzled that Paul does so here: '*my* patience, *my* love, *my* steadfastness.' We would rightly be offended if one of our Christian contemporaries set himself up as an example of Christian maturity, but remember that the circumstances are entirely different. The New Testament (along with the Old, Rom. 15:4; 1 Cor. 10:1–11) provides us with all the instruction we need, but in Timothy's day it was in process of compilation. It was both right and natural that the young minister should look to his senior colleague to exemplify in his life the truths he had proclaimed with his lips. Contrast these nine uplifting, inspiring and outgoing qualities with the nineteen selfish and ungodly characteristics mentioned at the beginning of the chapter. Paul repeats here something he has said earlier (1:8,12; 2:1–3), that no Christian worker can hope to escape suffering, and he provides his reader with an example (11) from that most memorable part of the first missionary journey, as far as Timothy was concerned, the time when the apostle visited his home territory (Acts 13 and 14; compare 16:1–5). These details recall Timothy's first meeting with Paul and now, as the apostle is about to leave this world, he reminds his colleague of their early contacts and continuing allegiance. Do we take the time to encourage those who first encouraged us? In the pressure of life it is all too easy to forget those to whom, spiritually, we are most indebted. Paul testifies here to three indisputable facts: (*a*) evil people will continue to emerge (13), (*b*) all who pursue godliness will encounter hardship (12), and (*c*) the Lord comes to the rescue of his persecuted people (11b; compare 4:17,18).

QUESTIONS: How would you define the apostle Paul's 'aim in life' (10)? What evidence is there for the 'aim' in this letter?

3:14–17 The plea for continuance

Mention of his ministry in Lystra (11) recalls for Paul his visit to the home of Eunice and the godly instruction Timothy had received from the Old Testament Scriptures since his earliest days (15). The influence of a Christian home is incalculable, and remember that it cannot have been easy for Eunice in that her husband certainly does not appear to have been a believer (Acts 16:1). It was a spiritually divided home but, undaunted by that disadvantage, Timothy's mother made sure that the young boy listened each day to the reading of Scripture. But, helpful as it is, a good spiritual upbringing is not enough. However much a man or woman may have 'learned' in the past, the believer must 'continue' in the faith if he wishes to be 'complete' or 'efficient' (*artios*, 17) and 'equipped', a 'workman able to set his hand to any task that confronts him' (Barrett).

In order to become a man or woman of God (17), the believer must make a really important place in his life for the study of God's Word. Notice that it is a saving Word (15b). The Old Testament, which young Timothy studied from childhood, pointed forward to the advent of Messiah. In its various parts that marvellous book spoke eloquently of the coming Christ (compare Luke 24:25–27,32), the suffering Redeemer (1 Pet. 1:10–12; 2:22–25; compare Isa. 53). The Old Testament is a book about the promised salvation. Holy Scripture is, moreover, a unique Word, 'inspired' (*theopneustos*, literally 'God-breathed'), words that were 'breathed out' by God himself, in Old Testament times, in the ministry of Jesus (1 Tim. 5:18, 'the scripture says') and in Paul's teaching (1 Cor. 2:13; 1 Thess. 2:13; 2 Pet. 3:15–16: 'the other scriptures'). Furthermore, these unique Scriptures are a 'profitable' word, unlike the destructive, harmful message of the imposters and heretics. They neither encourage nor minimise evil; they issue 'reproof' and correct it. This book is also an effective word. It provides a man with 'training in righteousness', discipline, or a spiritual education (16b, same word as in 2:25, '*correcting* his opponents'). Correction when we go wrong and equipment to enable us to do right – both are provided by this transforming Word. It is a book which makes its obedient readers different. The Christian worker who is regularly taught by the Word is best equipped for the work.

THOUGHT: Christian maturity is the fruit of continuing obedience. Remember Paul's counsel to young Timothy: 'Continue in what you have learned' (14).

4:1–5 Always be steady

Counterfeit teachers (3:8) and other corrupt people (3:2–5) will ultimately have to meet the one who will judge all men, living and dead (1). Timothy will also be accountable and Paul issues the young minister with a solemn 'charge' (*diamartyromai*, 'adjure', as a witness under oath in a court of law; compare 1 Tim. 5:21), solemnly and reverently calling as witnesses the Lord God and his only Son. The earnestness of this closing appeal is naturally heightened by the fact that the apostle knows his end is near.

Timothy is to be *a faithful messenger*; 'preach' (2) describes the activity of the herald who is commissioned to declare certain facts in the market–place; he is not free to proclaim his own ideas (like the false teachers) or adapt the message to his people's likings (3). His most serious responsibility is to pass on to others the word which has been given to him – nothing else and nothing less. He must be *an alert sentinel*: 'be urgent' (2, NEB margin, 'be on duty at all times'). This word is sometimes found in the papyri of a soldier on guard or a 'stand by', ready for action. He is to be *a patient teacher*. People will not always want to hear the instruction he is commissioned to share, but he will hand on the truth at times when they like it and on days when they don't (2). The negative aspects of his ministry in reproof and correction will hardly make him popular, but they are a necessary prelude to exhortation. Those who stubbornly continue in sin must be urged to forsake it before they can benefit by the appeal to do good. It is possible that 'in season . . . out' ('welcome or unwelcome', JB) refers to the teacher as well as to the hearers! John Stott believes we have here not 'an excuse for . . . insensitive brashness', but 'a biblical appeal against laziness'. Timothy must also be *a courageous sufferer* with the capacity for steady endurance (5a, recalling 2:12), a man who will 'keep calm and sane at all times' (NEB) even when he is most fiercely opposed. Finally, he must be *a tireless evangelist* (5b), constantly eager to bring others to Christ. With perseverance he must 'fulfil' this ministry – the word is used in Acts 12:25 when Paul and Barnabas completed their assignment.

THOUGHT: Timothy is here reminded that, however difficult the task, he must be 'unfailing in patience and in teaching'. The late fourth–century preacher, John Chrysostom, said: 'If fishermen do not despair, though often they cast their nets for a whole day without catching anything, much more should not we.'

Although Paul has just laid a solemn 'charge' (1) upon Timothy, he is not calling his 'son' to anything he has not already done himself. In his present circumstances he waits like an animal about to be sacrificed. His former sufferings (1:12; 2:9; 3:11) are but a prelude to the forthcoming 'offering' which is, literally, already being poured out (see 6, NEB, compare Phil. 2:17). In the past he has done all those things he expects of Timothy (7). Like a soldier he has 'fought' for Christ; as a disciplined, obedient athlete he has 'finished the race' and as a reliable steward he has played his part in keeping or guarding the deposit of the gospel. Truth to tell, 'the faith' had also kept him (John 17:11–15; 1 Thess. 5:23). Paul does not merely engage in reminiscences of days gone by; he anticipates a far more exciting and rewarding future. The apostle has already appeared before an unrighteous Roman judge, but he will yet appear before an entirely righteous Judge who will not order his execution but acknowledge his service (8). The coming Day is for Paul far more significant than the time of his 'departure' (6b, where the word used is one which describes the release of a boat untied from its moorings). In the course of life's voyage he has met many people. Some, like Timothy (9), were 'genuinely anxious' (Phil. 2:20) for the apostle's welfare. Others, like Demas, have dropped out of the race (10). Some, like Luke, had stayed alongside the apostle (11a); as a doctor what a help he must have been. After Mark's disappointing beginning in the work (Acts 13:13; 15:36–40), he was now a 'very useful' companion who, with Timothy (9,21), Paul would like to see again before the end (11b). Not everyone was either helpful or useful, of course. Apart from worldly (10) and other (16) deserters, like Demas and the rest, there were fierce opponents like Alexander (14). Paul's last word is not about himself, his friends or enemies, but about the Lord who will 'be with' Timothy (22) as he certainly had been with Paul as the unfailing Companion, strengthening Lord (17), invincible Helper, eternal Saviour and heavenly King (18).

THOUGHT: Apart from the familiar names mentioned here, there are others, not so well-known, but whose kindly ministry to Paul will be remembered in heaven: 'Pudens, Linus, Claudia and *all the brethren*'. Thank God for the great multitude of his loyal servants throughout the centuries whose names are never recalled, but whose deeds will never be forgotten.

Analysis of Titus

1:1–4	**Opening salutation**
1:5–9	**Blameless Leaders**
1:10–16	**Harmful Deceivers**
2:1–10	**Exemplary Members**
2:11–3:7	**The Unique Saviour**

	2:11–15	Redeems his people
	3:1–7	Renews his people

3:8–15	**Closing words**

	3:8	Exhortation
	3:9–11	Warning
	3:12–15	Greetings

1:1–4 Manifested in his word

Though hardly as well-known as Timothy, Titus was one of Paul's greatly valued helpers in the work. We have already seen his name in our last reading (2 Tim. 4:10); like Timothy, he is the apostle's 'true-born' (4, NEB) son. One of Paul's Gentile converts, Titus was the apostle's travelling companion when he went to Jerusalem (Gal. 2:1–3; compare Acts 15:2) and, after that delicate mission, Titus was himself sent on important journeys for Paul to the churches, e.g. 2 Cor. 2:13; 7:13–15; 8:6,16–18; 12:18. Paul trusted him with increasing responsibility, regarding him as his 'partner and fellow worker' (2 Cor. 8:23). He had been to Corinth (2 Cor. 7:6,7) and when our epistle opens we discover he has been serving in Crete (5). Later, he is sent to Nicopolis (3:12), still later to Dalmatia (2 Tim. 4:10). Widely travelled and greatly used, Titus is the kind of responsible leader who can be entrusted with a difficult task. Anyone who can complete a successful mission to a pathetically divided church like Corinth (1 Cor. 1:10–13; 5:1–7; 11:18–22; 15:12; 2 Cor. 2:1–4; 7:6–9) can certainly be trusted with even more demanding assignments! Paul left him in Crete where it was far from easy; the apostle realises that (5–12). It is all the more important therefore that this warm-hearted pastoral letter to a trusted friend should begin by focusing on the great centralities of the faith, the message which not only changes lives, but sustains them. He reminds Titus of the sovereign God who gathers his own 'elect' and therefore secure people (1), a reliable God who makes eternal promises and 'never lies' (2), a saving God (note 3, 'God our Saviour' and 4, 'Christ Jesus our Saviour') who has 'entrusted' Paul with this message of salvation (2:11) and a loving God, 'the Father' of all who believe in him. Paul regards himself as God's slave (1, margin), utterly at his disposal, Christ's apostle, sent to encourage and instruct God's people, the church's teacher (3) and Titus's spiritual father (4a). This letter tells us that we can 'further the faith of God's elect and their knowledge of the truth' (1) by preaching (3), correction (5), stability (9), example (2:7), dependabilty (2:10), holiness (2:12), pure conversation, courtesy (3:2) and love (3:15). Note how frequently these themes emerge in this short letter. The first reader was assured in its opening sentences of rich, available and limitless resources. God's grace and peace (4b) would never fail.

THOUGHT: Peace ('Shalom') was a familiar Jewish greeting, but 'Grace' is the ground on which *all* God's gifts are available to every believer. James Moffatt put it like this: 'All is of grace and grace is for all.'

1:5–16 The steward's work

Paul knows from his own experience that the churches are not likely to be effective spiritual agencies if their leadership is poor. The Cretan church seems to have been initially 'defective' in this respect (5) and one of Titus' responsibilities was that of appointing 'elders' and 'bishops' – the terms appear to be synonymous in this passage (5–7). 'Elders' may mean leaders generally, without specific reference to particular responsibilities. The qualifications necessary for the task recall similar detail in 1 Timothy 3:1–10, though there are some interesting additional details here worthy of note. In this passage the elder's family is singled out as a matter for special concern. Paul told Timothy to pay attention to that at Ephesus (1 Tim. 3:4,12), but the apostle says that in Crete Titus should see to it that the children of church leaders are also believers (6) and therefore not likely to be accused of either profligacy or insubordination, common sins on the island (12). In his travels Paul had realised time and again the importance of the home as a unit for faithful teaching, pastoral care, evangelistic opportunity, as well as family life. Contrast the unstable home in verse 11. Nowadays, when even some Christian marriages end in disaster, we do well to cultivate the ministry of the home. Parents need to give time to its development. The bishop's task is related here as well as his qualities; he is *God's* steward (7). As manager of God's affairs, he is responsible to his employer to do exactly what the Master orders or desires. This person must also be 'master of himself' (8) even when others around him (12) cannot control their tongues ('liars'), conduct ('evil beasts') and appetites ('gluttons'). From the church's leaders and the Christian home, Paul turns to false teachers. These garrulous (10), money-making (11b) heretics have a legalistic message (10, 'the circumcision party') with ascetical demands ('the commands of men', 14) and gnostic tendencies (v. 15 suggests that certain foods, practices, institutions, e.g. marriage, were considered 'impure'). It is interesting to see that, out of his well-stored mind, Paul could helpfully quote pagan authors like Epimenides (12), Aratus (Acts 17:28) and Menander (1 Cor. 15:33), as well as the Old Testament and the teaching of Jesus (1 Tim. 5:18). Calvin's comments on verse 12 make it clear that the apostle had little time for those who 'refuse to make any use of secular authors'.

THOUGHT: How awful to deny God by one's deeds (16). Contrast the leader who is 'a lover of goodness' (8) with the misleader who is 'unfit for any good deed' (16).

2:1–10 Belief and behaviour

Titus is not only a faithful teacher (1) but also a sensitive pastor, recognising that, at the various stages in life, men and women often need different counsel. The doctrine of God is not only to be proclaimed by tongue, but silently expounded in a consistent life (10). Elderly and mature Christian men ought to possess the qualities described in verse 2, though older people's relationships are not always marked by 'love' and in times of trial 'steadfastness' can elude even the elderly. The older women are to be reverent toward God, kind and truthful in what they say about others, and released from personal bondage to their lower nature (3). The mature Christian woman, rich in faith, has a great teaching opportunity which she can use to encourage younger women to develop a strong family life (4). These younger sisters in the fellowship (5) must not only be morally pure ('chaste'), industrious ('domestic' literally means 'working at home', compare 1 Tim. 5:13), compassionate ('kind' to others balances the house-proud, insular woman who rarely does anything for anyone else) and 'submissive' to their husbands (Col. 3:18). They must also be endowed with a strong sense of spiritual responsibility, determined that God's Word shall not be 'discredited' by unworthy behaviour. The younger men (6) are to be self-controlled. Paul instructs Titus about his personal life. Young as he is (implied in vs. 6,7), if he is to teach others (1), his own life must be 'a model' (7) of appropriate Christian living; the word used here (and in 1 Tim. 4:12, 'example') describes an impress of a die. C. K. Barrett makes an important point here: 'The moral claims laid upon rank-and-file Christians are substantially the same as those made elsewhere upon ministers. There is only one standard, though it is perhaps specially important that official and public persons should reach it.' The reference to 'slaves' (9) reminds us of the importance of everyday work as a sphere of life where the doctrine is to be adorned by our respect, the good quality of our service, our harmonious relationships with others, our honesty and complete dependability and trustworthiness – all these are in verses 9,10. These aspects of the Christian doctrine of work were demanded of those who were socially underprivileged, sometimes physically ill-treated and generally despised. Do not our greatly improved conditions of employment demand an even greater commitment to these principles?

THOUGHT: If, in adverse circumstances, Christian slaves were expected to 'adorn' the doctrine as beautifully arranged jewels (that is the meaning here), surely we can do the same.

2:11–15 Grace has appeared

That God's grace has appeared 'for *all* mankind' (11, NEB) may mean 'even for slaves' (see 9,10) and other despised or unwanted people, or it may be a conscious tilt at those false teachers on Crete and elsewhere who insist that 'salvation' (a favourite word in the gnostic vocabulary) is for the favoured few who have been secretly initiated into their exclusive privileges. These verses provide Titus with a remarkably full summary of Christian teaching. Unlike the 'Jewish myths' (1:14) and other speculative notions which were abroad at the time (1 Tim. 1:4; 4:7; 2 Tim. 4:4), true Christian doctrine has a firm historical foundation. God's grace, in the person of his Son Jesus Christ, 'has appeared' physically amongst men. He actually came to this world (some gnostic teachers denied that) at Bethlehem and, at the end of his earthly life he 'gave himself' (14) as our Redeemer. It all happened in time (1 Tim. 6:13) and can be verified. Moreover, Christian doctrine has essential moral implications. A man cannot accept this teaching and then live exactly as he likes. He must conform to this message's ethical demands. He cannot continue in his earlier irreligious ways and former ungodliness (12), but must have a new life-style. He renounces 'worldly passions', but still lives his transformed life 'in this world' (12). By contrast, some gnostics treasured the forlorn hope of a mystical flight away from the world into the realm of 'spirit' where one's ethical conduct was of no significance whatever. Furthermore, Christian doctrine has a heartening future dimension (13). The 'blessed hope' is clearly related to the ethical demands. Believers want to be at their best, morally and spiritually, when he returns (1 John 3:3). The 'hope' not only provokes holiness; it inspires confidence. In addition, Christian doctrine has rich corporate elements. Salvation is not individualistic, as the religiously self-satisfied gnostics maintained. Christ gave himself for *us*, to redeem *us* and to gather 'a people', purified, owned and used ('zealous for good deeds') by him (14). Finally, to return to the point with which we began, this treasured Christian doctrine has demanding evangelistic significance. He 'appeared for . . . all' (11). Christ was not 'given' for our sins only (1 John 2:2). A man like Titus, with this kind of message, would be first to acknowledge that it was to be widely declared (15) so that people could not carelessly ignore its demands ('reprove'), despise its authority, or 'disregard' its warnings conveyed through Crete's minister.

A REMINDER: Christians know that although their salvation is not a reward for 'good deeds', such zealous, outgoing, practical service is clearly expected of those who are God's 'people' (14).

3:1–15 Changed lives

In this closing section Paul first considers the Christian's attitude to society; he insists that believers must be reminded of truth they already know (see Rom. 13:1; 1 Pet. 2:13,14) about being 'submissive to the government' (1, NEB). Unlike some gnostic separatists or Cretan rebels (as described by Polybius, *History* VI.46.9), Christians are to respect the God-given authority of the state. In local society Christians must be good workers or (see NEB margin) 'ready always to do good', i.e. eager to express loyal citizenship in practical service to the community. Paul knows that little is more harmful and disruptive in human relationships than an uncontrolled tongue (2). Notice the importance of speech in this letter (1:10,12a; 2:3,8; 3:9). Courtesy (i.e. gentleness or 'meekness', same word as in Matt. 11:29; 21:5; 2 Cor. 10:1 describing Christ and in Matt. 5:5; Gal. 5:23 of Christians) must not be reserved for superiors or officials in authority, nor denied to those we find fractious or difficult. The apostle says that before we became Christians we were as bad as anyone else (3; compare Rom. 1:28–32; 2 Tim. 3:2–5). The account of what Jesus did for our salvation is a better story than what we did in our degradation. Verses 4–7 provide a highly compressed trinitarian confession of faith, majestic in grandeur, in which almost every other word cries out for exposition. Some scholars believe it may be a baptismal hymn. Underline what you believe to be the most significant terms in these verses and you will see how rich this teaching is which Titus is to expound (2:1) with integrity, gravity (2:7) and confidence (8, 'affirm confidently', RV). God initiated our salvation (4); Christ obtained it (5a) and the Holy Spirit effects it (5b–7). There may be a reference here (8) to a Christian's attitude to work where NEB reads 'engage in honourable occupations' (see RSV margin also) and if so, it recalls 2:9,10, but most scholars believe that verses 8 and 14 refer to compassionate service to others. As to church relationships (9–11), Titus must avoid profitless controversy and insist (8; compare 1 Tim. 1:7, 'make assertions', same word) on the great centralities of the faith (4–7). The quarrelsome member must be disciplined (10; compare Matt. 18:15–17). The closing verses remind us of Paul's indebtedness to his colleagues (12,13), the world's need of love (14) and the promise of sufficient grace for everyone (15).

THOUGHT: Paul emphasises that his message is about what our triune God has done for us, yet he applies these doctrines to everyday life in Crete and elsewhere. Our 'good deeds' (8) can never be the right means of procuring salvation, but they will always be the best method for expressing it.

Questions for further study and discussion on 2 Timothy 3:10 – Titus 3:15

1. Even in prison under the daily threat of execution, Paul valued the opportunity to read and write (2 Tim. 4:13). The 'parchments' (either his favourite Scriptures or blank pages) were more important than the winter cloak (13, see v. 21). Consider the creative use of time for someone confined to their home. List the possibilities. How might Christ's work be extended by their enforced restrictions?

2. Re-read 2 Timothy 4:9–22 and, as an act of thanksgiving to the Lord, make a list of the people who have been the greatest help to you in your Christian life. Do they all know about it? Some of them may well fear that they have never been of significant help to anyone. Your encouragement could provide a necessary spur for further witness or service.

3. In some parts of our world, where the freedom to evangelise is either restricted or denied, it is difficult for Christians to reconcile teaching like Titus 3:1 (compare Rom. 13:1–5; 1 Pet. 2:13,14,17b) with sayings like Acts 4:18–20, 27–29. How would you set about resolving the problem?

4. The letter to Titus is particularly rich in its doctrine of God. Make a study of God's nature, word and people in this epistle.

5. Paul frequently emphasises in these letters, and elsewhere, the importance of his example. How important is the example of more mature Christians? How far could we, should we, encourage new Christians to model themselves on others?

6. What can we learn from the Pastoral epistles about bringing up children?

7. What principles do we find here which are applicable to our lives at work? How should Christians stand out in their attitudes?

8. How have you found the Scriptures to be 'profitable'? How does your experience compare with Paul's teaching (2 Tim. 3:16,17)?

Analysis of Philemon

1–7 Love at work

This fascinating little letter, full of human interest, is a spiritual treasure. Some early Christian writers wondered whether it ought to have been included in the Canon because it was so private and commonplace – but we can be very grateful that it was. It reminds us that our gospel is about real life in the everyday world. Although the letter is, as Luther says, 'a purely private and domestic one', it deals with great doctrinal themes in the context of the sharply divided, often ruthless, world of the first century where there was an immense chasm between slave and freeman, Jew and Gentile, male and female. This priceless letter crosses all those deep gulfs of enmity, suspicion and isolation. The freeman appeals on behalf of the slave; the Jew cares about the Gentile; the man expresses his indebtedness to the woman (2) whose home has housed the local church. Paul is firm in his confidence; he is Christ's (not Caesar's) prisoner (1; Rom. 8:28; Phil. 1:12–14). A sovereign God does not make mistakes. There is purpose even in persecution. Moreover, Paul is blessed in his friendships (1,2,23,24). In various parts of the Roman world there are believers who love him and whose homes are open to him (22). Do other Christians derive inspiration from the quality of our compassionate service for others (7)? Paul is also controlled by his gospel. Before coming to his specific request about Onesimus, he mentions a number of spiritual truths which clearly determine his approach to the delicate matter he is about to raise. He approaches Philemon on the basis of their common faith (5,6). They are committed to the same good news with its message of promised reconciliation, restored relationships, undeserved generosity and creative peace. Paul can seek Philemon's help on the basis of their mutual love (5,7). Love reached Paul when he was a different kind of runaway, when enmity controlled his passions and bitterness drove him on (Acts 8:1–3; 9:1,2; 26:9–11). The man who was once a rebel (see Rom. 5:10) could do nothing else but ask that another sinner might be loved and trusted (Acts 9:17, 26,27). Paul also approached Philemon on the basis of their deepening understanding of the Christian faith (6). He knew that 'all the good that is ours in Christ' is not likely to be disclosed fully in one flash of overwhelming revelation either on the Damascus Road or anywhere else. A shared (*koinōnia*) faith will not only spread it more widely (a possible interpretation of v. 6a), but more deeply too, so that people discern its practical implications and unlimited resources.

QUESTION: Are 'the hearts of the saints . . . refereshed through you' (7)?

8–25 Made useful

Although these verses contain a down-to-earth, practical request (15–19), they also expound some of the leading elements in Paul's gospel. It is a gospel of compassionate action (8–10). It moved beyond words to deeds. Christ did not simply preach; he healed and gave himself as a sacrifice. So 'for love's sake' the apostle asks Philemon to listen to his plea on behalf of the man who, like Timothy and Titus, has become another of Paul's spiritual children (10). Paul's appeal (9, either as an old man, *presbutēs*, deserving respect, or as an 'ambassador', *presbeutēs*, claiming authority) is grounded in his gospel, a message about forgiveness and restoration for those who least deserve it. It is also a gospel of radiant optimism (11–14). Whatever the difficulties, things can be different. Paul had been changed from a persecutor to a preacher. Onesimus could be changed from a useless thief (18) to a beneficial colleague (13). Philemon could change too, from understandable resentment to brotherly affection (16). Luther maintained that this is why Philemon has been given a place in the New Testament: 'Thus no one ought to despair about anyone else.' It reminds one of John Wycliffe's statement that no one commits blasphemy against the Holy Spirit but he who sins by finally despairing.

Paul believed in a gospel of deepening relationships (15,16). In a world where slaves and women counted for little, he reckoned both to be his brothers and sisters. Notice Paul's references to his or Philemon's brothers. Finally, Paul was encouraged by a gospel of supportive partnership (17–25). If Philemon regarded Paul as a 'partner' (*koinōnon*), then he would surely give the runaway the same loving welcome he would have extended to the apostle. There are other partners here too (23,24), in this best of all work, besides the one who opened his home (2, 22a), shared his faith (5,6), demonstrated his love (5,7) and offered his prayers (22b): Epaphras, who earnestly prayed for others (Col. 4:12,13) even in a prison cell; Mark, further proof of the power of Christ to change defectors (Acts 13:13; 15:37–39), effect reconciliation and make a disappointing man 'useful' (2 Tim. 4:11b); Luke, a lovable colleague in the work (Col. 4:14); and Demas.

THOUGHT: Calvin says that Demas' name must ever be a warning: 'if one of Paul's assistants . . . was afterwards drawn away . . . let none of us rely too much on our own zeal lasting even one year, but remembering how much of the journey still lies ahead, let us ask God for steadfastness' (see 2 Tim. 4:9,10).

Hebrews : Introduction

Written by an author who does not choose to identify himself, this 'letter' reads more like a sermon (13:22), carefully prepared in order to be read to a particular congregation. Its first readers, probably Jewish Christians, appear to be in danger of slipping back into reliance on their former ceremonial observances. Under the pressure of Jewish hostility, some may even have denied the deity of Christ and the uniqueness of his saving work. Well-acquainted with the Greek version of the Old Testament, the Septuagint, our author regularly cites Old Testament Scripture to support his argument that the ceremonial law of earlier times was but a temporary measure, designed primarily to educate the Hebrew people rather than effect the inward cleansing which every worshipper knew to be necessary.

There has been increased interest in this epistle since the discovery of the Dead Sea Scolls and the light they have shed on the first–century religious community at Qumran. These devout Jewish believers seem to have been led by a group of priests who, spiritually dissatisfied with normative Judaism, had left the Jerusalem Temple to establish a distinctive community life and faith in the wilderness of Judea. The suggestion has been made that it may have been this kind of more 'spiritual' type of Judaism which had influenced the first recipients of this letter rather than that taught by the rabbis. It may be a pure coincidence, but many of the themes developed in Hebrews, like the function of angels, the new covenant teaching of Jeremiah 31, the role of Melchizedek, the place of ceremonial washings, are also central in the teaching of the Scrolls. This Qumran group had gone to the desert determined to model their daily life on the pattern of the Israelite pilgrims in the wilderness under the leadership of Moses centuries earlier. They were preparing for a time when they would re-enter a purified Jerusalem and resume, under the leadership of a new high priest, the original Mosaic sacrificial system. They anticipated the coming of two outstanding figures with messianic functions, a kingly and a priestly leader, both of whom would be subordinate to Michael the archangel. The 'world to come' (2:5) would thus be subjected to angelic authority. It is easy to see how this letter, with its insistence on the uniqueness of Christ and his supremacy over angels, Moses and Aaron, would have immediate relevance and appeal. In the words of one of this letter's most recent commentators, this Qumran background is 'undoubtedly the best theory yet advanced to explain the occasion and purpose' of the letter. 'It is a key which seems quite remarkably to fit the lock and open a door that has for so long remained closed' (Philip Hughes).

Analysis of Hebrews

1:1–2:10	**The Word of God**	
	1:1–14	The unique Word: Christ's diety
	2:1–4	Warning against neglecting the word of the gospel
	2:5–10	The personified Word: Christ's humanity
2:11–6:20	**The Call of God**	
	2:11–18	The word of deliverance
	3:1–6	The word of assurance
	3:7–4:13	The word of warning
	4:14–5:10	The word of sensitive compassion
	5:11–6:8	The word which aids maturity
	6:9–20	The word which inspires hope
7:1–10:18	**The Work of Christ**	
	7:1–14	Christ's uniqueness
	7:15–8:5	Christ's priesthood
	8:6–9:5	Christ's covenant
	9:6–10:18	Christ's sacrifice
10:19–13:19	**The Life of Faith**	
	10:19–25	Its corporate nature
	10:26–31	Its deliberate rejectors
	10:32–11:40	Its valiant examples
	12:1–3	Its supreme initiator
	12:4–17	Its disciplinary aspect
	12:18–29	Its unique privileges
	13:1–19	Its practical consequences
13:20–25	**Benediction and closing salutation**	

1:1–4 The unique Christ

This opening section, written in magnificent Greek, reads more like the beginning of a sermon than the introduction to a letter; the frequent exhortations (2:1; 3:1,12,13; 4:1,11,14; 6:1) indicate that this is the work of a dedicated pastoral preacher concerned not only to teach (see 5:11–6:2), but eager to elicit a response from his readers. His main themes of revelation and redemption are both compressed into this introductory passage. Before dealing with his readers' problems, he reminds them of the majestic glory and sufficiency of Christ. He has spoken God's *Word* more eloquently than anyone else and has accomplished God's *work* as the unique and effective redeemer of enslaved mankind (2:15). His love of Old Testament Scripture is to become increasingly evident, but he announces at the beginning that Christians rejoice in a God who declares his truth (1,2a), reveals his nature (2b,3a) and achieves his saving purposes in his only Son, the Lord Jesus Christ.

The letter's first readers were in danger of returning to their earlier commitment to Jewish faith and practice, so forsaking Christ; this exposition of his uniqueness reflects great pastoral skill in helping his spiritually hesitant readers by pointing them to Jesus. Inadequate views about Christ are likely to lead not only to spiritual frustration but utter disaster. God's love and unchanging patience are demonstrated by his use of different ways (1) to communicate his message in earlier times – prophets, patriarchs, priests, kings, wise men, psalmists. The rich variety of the Old Testament revelation is forcefully illustrated in the letter's many quotations. God's power was also manifest in the created order. His word did not simply announce facts; it effected what he said (Gen. 1:3). Jesus, as God's pre-existent Son, shared in creation (John 1:3; Col. 1:16); moreover, he continues to sustain it by his equally powerful word (3a). God's perfect nature has been clearly seen in Jesus and the Father's transcendent glory shines through Christ's spotless life (3; compare Matt. 17:2; John 1:14; 2 Cor. 4:6). God is uniquely present among men (John 14:8–11) in the person of his Son. But we are unclean rebels, loving the darkness of our sin rather than the pure, convicting light of his divine person. We need to be purified by him (3b) before we can be surrendered to, or used by, him. His finished and effective work of cleansing and salvation is to become the dominant theme of this letter's central section.

THOUGHT: 'When he had made purification for sins, he sat down at the right hand of the Majesty on high' (3). 'With this brief word he makes useless absolutely all the righteousnesses and deeds of penitence of men. But he praises the exceedingly great mercy of God' (Luther).

1:5–14 Far above angels

Under pressure of persecution, some of our writer's Jewish Christian readers were in danger of exchanging their earlier firm convictions about the deity of Christ for another view which might allow them to remain within the secure confines (and social acceptability) of Judaism. If Jesus was only a very special messenger (*angelos*) from God, and not his unique Son, then it might be possible for them to keep one foot in the church and the other in the local synagogue. The pressures of increasing religious hostility are illustrated within the pages of the New Testament (Acts 4:1–3; 5:17,18; 6:8–8:3; 9:13,14; 14:1–7,19; Rev. 2:9,10; 3:9,10) and many Christians must have been tempted to compromise their faith in the superiority and uniqueness of Jesus. The problem is certainly not peculiar to the ancient world; in our own day, with its popular religious pluralism, there are those who want a Christ who is only human and scarcely 'divine' in any sense other than that which they see in outstanding leaders in other faiths. Our author rightly insists here that Jesus is far more than a special 'messenger', the highest angel, sent to deliver the finest message.

He quotes the Word of God in order to exalt the Son of God. Most of those who argue today against Christ's deity also doubt the unique value, trustworthiness and authority of God's Word. If we doubt the Scripture, we shall soon reject the Son of whom it constantly speaks (Luke 24:27). Throughout Old Testament history God was pleased to use angels to communicate truth, issue warnings and effect deliverance, but they are his creatures and not to be worshipped (see Col. 2:18), whereas Christ is the Son of God (5) whom both we and the angels adore (6). They are servants (7), but he is the sovereign Son (note the coronation symbolism in vs. 8,9). He shared as God's agent in creation (10), which included the creation of the angels as well as the heaven and earth. The universe, angels and mankind all belong to the realm of the perishable order, but he remains (12) as the exalted, victorious Son who sits at the Father's right hand, his saving work complete (13). The angels serve the people of God (14), but only the Son saves them. Angels may speak about salvation (Matt. 1:20,21; Luke 2:9–14) and rejoice when individuals are saved (Luke 15:10), but they could not possibly have accomplished this eternally effective work. Only Christ could do that.

THOUGHT: The praises of Jesus the angels proclaim,
Fall down on their faces, and worship the Lamb.
(Charles Wesley)

2:1–4 Serious neglect

The angels (1:4–14) provide a link with the practical exhortation which is now before us. They played a part in the transmission of the Jewish law (2, compare Acts 7:53; Gal. 3:19) and if disobedience of the law was punished, how can we escape if we despise or ignore the message of salvation? This passage expounds one of our writer's themes, the Word of God and our obedience to it. These first–century readers must pay careful attention to this message and not let it slip, as a ring slips easily from a finger or a boat drifts away from its moorings (some other uses of the word used in v. 1). It seems that some of his readers had hardened their hearts to the divine voice (3:7–12), the word which had living power and could expose hidden motives as well as more obvious sins (4:12,13). Because they were lethargic ('dull of hearing') and apathetic about their spiritual food, they had neither received help for their own lives nor had they been able to impart truth to others (5:11,12). Remaining as spiritual infants (5:13; compare 1 Pet. 2:2), they had not progressed to mature Christian experience and so were scarcely able to discern good and helpful things from those which were evil and damaging (5:13,14).

No wonder, at this early point in the letter, the members of the congregation are urged to give themselves whole-heartedly to a careful study of God's Word and an obedient response to the claims of God's Son. Notice the trinitarian reference here. *Christ* declared God's truth (3) in his proclamation of the good news. *God* testified to the reliability of the apostolic gospel by giving unique 'signs' of its authenticity (4) and the *Holy Spirit* distributed various gifts to enable the message to become intimately known and widely believed. These gifts of preaching, teaching, serving, evangelism (Rom. 12:6–8; Eph. 4:7,11) are generously made available to the people of God, not for personal self-satisfaction, but for the blessing of others (1 Pet. 4:10,11). The sovereign Spirit distributed them 'according to his own will' (4), not according to ours. These first–century readers were in danger of allowing the vessel of their faith to be carried along by alien currents which would lead them into perilous waters. They must see that their faith is anchored to the objective, saving and life-imparting truth of God's word (Jas. 1:21; 1 Pet. 1:22–25) and is not a mere copy of the changing, subjective experiences of men.

THOUGHT: When men and women persist in neglecting life's greatest issue, that of their eternal salvation, they dismiss the fact that everyone is accountable to God and invite the condemnation of a caring Father.

2:5–9 We see Jesus

The author lingers with the theme of 'angels' throughout chapter 2 (5,7,9,16), though only because it provides him with an opportunity to exalt Christ and make further affirmations about his superiority over the angels. Many first-century religious people were persuaded that man's present life and future destiny were under the immediate control of angelic powers. Chapter 2:1–4 is a brief word of practical application rightly following up the teaching of chapter 1 and pressing home the need for concentrated attention on, and obedience to, the written and living Word of God. To catch the flow of the argument we need to miss out this extremely important digression in verses 1–4.

This letter asserts that man's present and future life is certainly not under the control of angels. All 'principalities and powers', good and evil, are subject to the sovereign Lord of history (Rom. 8:38,39; 1 Pet. 3:22). The 'world to come' (5) of which the writer has been speaking refers to the 'last days' (1:2; compare 6:5), the day of salvation (Luke 4:16–21; 2 Cor. 6:2) which had dawned with the coming of Christ and his gospel. Our entrance into this new life and new world is not subject to the authority of angels but to the generous mercy of God, the effective sacrifice of Christ and the continuing ministry of the Spirit. Christ rules, not the angels. He is 'crowned with glory and honour' (9), uniquely fulfilling in history man's original destiny (spoilt by sin). The description of the ideal man in Psalm 8 is here used (6–8) to portray the unique Son of Man. Man is not what he was meant to be (8b), with dominion over the rest of creation. Because of sin his life is one of shame and degradation (not glory and honour), bringing him in the end face to face with the ultimate fruit of his transgression and final consequence of his iniquity: death (15) and inevitable judgement (9:27). In order to save man Christ came and, although far above the angels, was willing to be made 'for a little while' lower than the angels (9) so that he might bear our sin (9:28; 1 Pet. 2:24) and put it away (9:26) by his unique sacrificial death. By God's grace (9) he entered not only the experience of death 'for every one', but also suffered the anguish of separation from his holy Father (Matt. 27:46) as he shed his blood for us (9:11–14).

THOUGHT: Believers are released from the fear of death because they know that Christ has entered fully into its suffering (9) and triumphed victoriously over its power. 'Who shall separate us from the love of Christ?' (Rom. 8:35)

2:10–18 The conqueror and his work

To obtain our deliverance (15) Christ had to become the *pioneer*, who opens up the trail and goes on ahead of us into the presence of God, making possible the entrance of his sons into eternal glory. But how could the sinless (7:26) Christ be made 'perfect through suffering'? Our writer does not refer here to the moral perfection of Jesus, but to the necessary fulfilment on earth of his divinely appointed destiny. Although in eternity Christ was perfectly at one with the Father and eager to do his will (10:7,9), that unique vocation as man's Saviour had to be worked out in history. The perfectly conceived plan had to be brought to a perfect fulfilment and God knew that the only 'fitting' (10) way of doing that in the life and ministry of his Son was by the way of suffering, death and resurrection. In the course of his earthly life Christ brought to perfection his vocation, his complete obedience to God, his identification with sinners and his victory over sin and death. Through this unique work of Christ sinful mankind is sanctified (11–13), 'set apart' for God's own use as his special instruments in the world. Sanctification is an important theme in this letter (10:10,14,29). Just as Jesus set himself apart for God's saving purposes in the world (9), so we are to be completely his; holy partners, his redeemed brothers (11,12), as well as God's children (13). Note that the psalm (Ps. 22) quoted here was in the mind and on the lips of Jesus as he suffered and then tasted death for us (Mark 15:34). Through Christ's death man is released from one of his worst fears, that of death, and from the enslaving power of the devil who constantly makes use of this 'fear of death' as he threatens men and women with its inevitability and finality. To achieve this, Christ took our nature upon himself (14,17) that he might effect our release from the power of sin, death and the devil (14,15). The best of angels could not have achieved that (16); they belong to a totally different order of created beings and cannot possibly *feel* in themselves what it is to be human. Jesus knows and for that reason, in addition to his saving work in the past, he helps us by his present work; totally committed to 'the service of God' (17), he perfectly sympathises with the daily needs of men and women.

THOUGHT: Touched with a sympathy within,
He knows our feeble frame;
He knows what sore temptations mean,
For He has felt the same.
(Isaac Watts)

3:1–6 The household of faith

The exhortation in these verses flows naturally from the teaching of the previous passage. We are 'holy brethren' (1); 'holy' because of our sanctification in Christ, and 'brethren' (compare 2:11; 3:12; 10:19) because in his Word he chooses to describe us in these terms of intimate and unending relationship. We are urged to 'consider' or continuously rivet our attention on Jesus, described here by a dual title, that of 'apostle' (the one sent from God to mankind) and 'high priest' (the one who represents mankind before God). Remember that these first–century Jewish Christian readers were in serious danger of fixing their attention on legalistic works (9:14), or on their treasured social and domestic privileges as members of Jewish communities and families, or on the religious security they enjoyed within the local synagogue and its traditions, rather than on Christ the only Saviour. Before we condemn them we need to remember that we too may be exposed to similar perils. Do we sometimes rely on our religious heritage, subjective spiritual experiences, orthodox doctrinal convictions or 'good works' – all not only proper but necessary within appropriate contexts, but not as substitutes for Christ? There is no other foundation (1 Cor. 3:11) and we can only be saved by repentance toward God and faith in Jesus (Acts 4:12).

These Jewish Christian readers must have felt acutely their enforced sense of separation from a Judaism now hostile, but in whose tradition in they had been lovingly nurtured and given a lively sense of God's majesty, holiness and mercy. They had belonged to his 'house', his household or beloved community. Were they now to lose all that rich sense of security and solidarity with God's people manifest in their rich and illuminating past? Our writer assures them that Moses, their great spiritual leader and teacher, was but a worker in this 'household'. Christ is its builder. They do not in any sense cut themselves off from this past; they must realise that Jesus has brought this priceless heritage to perfect fulfilment. They are the true 'descendants of Abraham' (2:16). Moses was a servant, but Jesus is the Son. Those words of ringing certainty must have brought renewed hope and a deeper commitment to many Jewish Christians in the first-century world: 'And *we* are his house.' We are joyfully secure as we 'hold fast' to that.

THOUGHT: Barclay comments that the invitation here (1) uses the same word as in Christ's exhortation that we '*consider* the ravens'. It is not merely to observe, but to 'look at the ravens and *understand and learn* the lessons God is seeking to teach you through them'.

Questions for further study and discussion on Philemon and Hebrews 1:1–3:6

1. What does the letter to Philemon and its message of reconciliation have to say to us in our sharply divided late twentieth-century society with its wide economic chasm between Western affluence and Third World poverty, its racial barriers, and religious differences and social divisions?

2. Paul prayed that Philemon's faith, as it was shared with others, would further people's understanding of 'all the good that is ours in Christ' (6). Attempt an identification and exposition of those 'good' things as they emerge in this short letter.

3. Read Hebrews 1 over again and then explain *how* Jesus is superior to the angels.

4. How would you use the teaching of the first two chapters of Hebrews in a discussion with a person who genuinely wanted to find faith in God, but was hesitant about accepting the deity of Christ?

5. How do we reconcile the statement that by his victorious death Christ destroyed the devil (Heb. 2:14) with other passages in Scripture (2 Cor. 2:11; 4:4; Jas. 4:7; 1 Pet. 5:8,9) and our own experience, which suggest that the enemy is very much alive?

6. How do these early chapters of Hebrews help us to face temptation?

7. These early Jewish Christians were in danger of giving greater importance to angels and Moses than to Jesus. What are the parallel dangers today? How can we combat them?

8. What does 3:1–6 say about the 'personality cult' that sometimes surrounds Christian leaders?

3:7–11 Hear his voice

This letter's first readers are urged to rejoice in the secure confidence that, through faith in Christ, they belong to God's house (6). Given this assurance, they can and must 'hold fast' to their earlier spiritual commitment and not throw it away (10:35) in time of testing. In chapter 2 he used Psalm 8 to expound his convictions about the submission of Christ as the perfect man; now he uses another psalm to illustrate the rebellion of sinful man during the period of the wilderness wanderings. Psalm 95 is most apposite here, with its portrayal of God as the Saviour, Creator and Shepherd of his people. But man is a rebel, determined to persist in his sinful disobedience or turn from God in blatant unbelief. In the Temple worship, the use of this psalm had ensured that the historical events of the wilderness rebellion (Exod. 17:1–7; Num. 20:1–13) were constantly recalled and recited as a warning about man's stubborn and self-centred nature. 1 Corinthians 10:1–11 is a passage with a similar message and aim where, once again, the wilderness wanderings are used as a vehicle of warning about the disobedience of professing Christians.

Think how important is the use of Old Testament Scripture by our author. These Jewish Christians must not think for a moment that they have been cut off from the great treasures of their history and unique revelation. Far from it; these familiar Old Testament stories and sayings have *added*, not diminished, meaning. They convey God's present message to his people. The Spirit of God continues to speak through these stories and sayings. This is what the Holy Spirit now *says* (7), not simply what he once *said*. In those distant days when God's people travelled through the wilderness *en route* to the promised land, their faith and confidence in God was shaken and, unhappily, during such times, the Hebrew pilgrims hardened their hearts and provoked God's displeasure. They went 'astray' (10) and ignored the way God had planned for them. The significance of this warning to the first readers of this letter is both clear and compelling. In difficult times they too could be guilty of disobedience to God's Word and the rejection of his divinely appointed way of salvation.

THOUGHT: *'Today*, when you hear his voice, do not harden your hearts' (7,8). How important it is not only to set aside a definite time in each day when that unique voice can be *heard* in Scripture, but also applied to our lives and obeyed.

3:12–19 Sin never keeps its promises

How is the danger of an evil, unbelieving heart to be avoided? This passage offers some important clues. We are urged, first of all, to 'take care' (12). Just to be aware of the danger is to be on the alert. Some professing Christians allow their spiritual lives to drift on; they rarely give thought to the possibility of dangerous rocks and quicksands. Moreover, there is a summons here to honest self-examination. These readers are urged to look carefully at their own lives 'lest there be in *any* of you' a sinful, unbelieving or disloyal heart.

Some readers of this letter have been naturally puzzled by the author's statement that for these Jewish Christians to turn their backs on Christ and return to Judaism is to 'fall away from the living God'. Surely, as devout Jews, they still believed in God! But it is important to understand that the rejection of Christ is an act of rebellion against the Father who sent his only Son for our salvation. Furthermore, we must remember that this letter began by asserting that the Lord Jesus is God's complete and final revelation (1:1–3). Rich as it is, the Old Testament revelation, on its own, is fragmentary, partial and unfinished. We cannot see God as he really is if we ignore Jesus. Christ is actually given the name 'God' in the opening chapter (1:8). So, for these readers to forsake their distinctively Christian commitment and withdraw, for social or religious reasons, back into the 'Jewishness' of their faith, is to become apostate by turning away from the living God as he has been clearly and uniquely revealed in the person of Christ.

But more than introspective self-examination is necessary. Christian experience is personal, but not individualistic. Just as verse 12 contains a warning about ourselves which 'marks the reality and urgency of the danger' (Westcott), so verse 13 urges us to minister each day to the needs of *other* believers so that we help to keep our Christian friends from harm (compare 10:25). A further issue here of great importance is that we are not likely to apostasise if we have a realistic view of the seriousness of sin. It is both alluring and deceitful (13b). As Samuel Rutherford wrote from prison in the early seventeenth century, 'the more sense of sin, the less sin'.

THOUGHT: The Israelites had a good leader (16), but a poor sense of personal commitment. We have more than a leader. Our partner (14a, literally, 'we still are partners of Christ') is our Saviour, and as we 'hold fast' we are 'guarded' (1 Pet. 1:5).

4:1–13 Promised rest

The story of the Exodus pilgrims continues to be used here as a parable of necessary warning. Our writer knows that they too heard the good news of redemption, but did not commit themselves entirely into the hands of their merciful and powerful Saviour-God. They became disloyal, disobedient, idolatrous, quarrelsome grumblers (Exod. 14:11,12; 16:2,3,7,8; 17:2–4,7; 18:15–18; 32:1–33:6) and the rest that was promised remained only a dream, simply because they did not put their complete trust in God (2). Psalm 95 is quoted again here and our author insists that the land of Canaan was certainly not the promised 'rest' of God for, years after the pilgrims' children entered the land, the psalmist continued to anticipate the 'rest' of God as something yet to be possessed (9).

This passage is a superb example of the perfect balance found in Scripture. Several passages in this letter insist on our strenuous continuance in faith; we must 'hold our first confidence firm to the end' (3:14). But the other essential aspect of faith is also stressed here. The 'sabbath rest' of God's people is like the rest which God experienced after the work of creation (4,10). Our salvation is not obtained by self-effort, but by 'entering in' to what God has already achieved for us and by receiving that work of new creation (2 Cor. 5:17) as a divine gift. It is certainly not a question of choosing between salvation either by unaided effort or by effortless faith. True New Testament 'faith' gives constant expression to its reality and genuineness by its evident manifestation of 'works'. The two are held together in biblical teaching about salvation and sanctification. Total preoccupation with our personal spiritual responsibility can issue in despairing frustration; exclusive concentration on 'salvation without effort' can lead to appalling complacency. Cessation from the labour to obtain our *present* rest (assured salvation, 10) must be accompanied by an earnest desire to press on towards the *ultimate* rest which God has prepared for all his people in eternity. Effective pilgrimage is possible because of God's powerful Word (12) which is able to achieve what is promised. Christians rejoice in the assurance that the God who has called them in Christ knows everything about them (13) and is well aware that they need the help of a praying and supporting partner (14–16).

THOUGHT: I cannot work my soul to save,
For that my Lord has done;
But I will work like any slave
For love of God's dear Son.

4:14–16 Always able to sympathise

The omniscient God (13) knows the hidden recesses of our minds; like a sharp sword (12; Eph. 6:17) his penetrating Word exposes our secret motives and discerns between what is superficial and what is real. Knowing us as well as he certainly does, our merciful God realises that we cannot make this pilgrimage to eternity on our own, even though we may be sincere believers with a genuine love for the things of God. We not only need a perfect Saviour (2:10) who has died for us (2:9,14), but a present helper (2:18) who lives (7:25) to provide increasing strength as the journey proceeds.

At this point in his masterly exposition of the person and work of Christ, our writer begins to expand and explain the statement made in the letter's introductory paragraph, that when Jesus 'had made purification for sins, he sat down at the right hand of the Majesty on high' (1:3). Jesus is our 'great High Priest' and he is able to help us because of his victorious sacrifice. He has 'passed through the heavens' (14). The ascension of Christ occupies a more central place in our writer's thinking than the resurrection, which is only mentioned twice (7:16; 13:20). The fact that Jesus has ascended to the throne of God is convincing evidence that his redemptive work is complete; he is *seated* in heaven, proof that his work is finished. The Old Testament priests had to *stand* in God's presence as their work was always unfinished (10:11,12). He supports us on the basis of what he has so perfectly done. But it is not all in the past; we need his present help and that too is assured. The one who has 'passed through the heavens' is a perfect man who, having lived in this world, knows the strains and stresses of our human existence. Though he is sinless, he knows what it is to be tempted. Though he is strong, he feels for the weak (15). Confident of his perfect eternal victory and his continuing sympathy, we must prove his complete adequacy, and we do that in the place of prayer. In that place we give daily expression to our dependence. Without prayer we are practical atheists. When we do not pray we are silently testifying to our own self-reliance. At the 'throne of grace' we are assured of abundant mercy (to cover our past sins) and sufficient grace (to meet our present needs).

THOUGHT: **Have we trials and temptations?**
Is there trouble anywhere?
We should never be discouraged:
Take it to the Lord in prayer!
What a profound relief and strong support to realise that 'Jesus knows our every weakness'.

5:1–10 Our obedient Lord

Those who served as priests in Old Testament times were glad to minister to the needs of their contemporaries. Such men were often painfully aware of their own weaknesses (2). They were just as much in need as the most sinful members of their congregations. Our writer has already made it clear that, without having sinned (4:15; 7:26), Jesus 'can deal gently with the ignorant and wayward' far better than any member of the Levitical priesthood. Important as Christ's sympathy is, however, that is not the main reason for his assumption of this unique priestly office. The Old Testament priests had to be appointed by God (1) and Jesus also was 'called by God' (4), and not self-appointed, to his mission as our eternal High Priest (5,6).

Verses 7–10 remind us that our writer is not simply concerned about Christ's present intercessory ministry in heaven. It is a matter of immense importance to him that Christ actually lived in this world. If he had not lived here on earth *then*, he could hardly help us in heaven *now*. There is more about the earthly life of Jesus in the letter to the Hebrews (1:2,3; 2:3,9,14,17–18; 7:14; 12:2–3; 13:12,20) than in any other New Testament writing, apart from the Gospels. Here the author takes us into the garden of Gethsemane; we are with Christ during the most agonising moments of his earthly life. If some of the readers of this letter were experiencing suffering, isolation, social ostracism, persecution and pain, they must think about Jesus who, in his darkest hour, did what they are to do (4:16); he prayed. His obedience to the Father's will in heaven had to be worked out and proved by his daily costly obedience on earth (8).

How was the eternally perfect Son of God 'made perfect' (9)? This is an aspect of Christ's person and work mentioned earlier in the letter (2:10). It is so that he might be 'fully qualified to be the Saviour and High Priest of his people' (F. F. Bruce). Jesus had to be appointed by God (5), identified with men (2:14,17), victorious over temptation (2:18; 4:15), willing to die for sinners (2:9,14,15; 9:11–14) and then be exalted to the right hand of God (1:3; 10:12). The ascension was his final qualification; this great act of divine vindication perfected his saving work for rebellious mankind.

THOUGHT: Obedience is not only a characteristic of Christ's life; it is an essential aspect of ours. Salvation is for 'all who obey him' (9).

5:11–6:3 You ought to be teachers

Our 'fully qualified' Saviour has been designated by God as the Christian's High Priest 'after the order of Melchizedek' (10). Our writer wants to explain what he means by that statement, but fears that his readers, being 'dull of hearing' (11), will not be able to take it in. This causes him to digress from his Melchizedek teaching and not return to it until 6:20. We have already noticed that revelation and redemption are his twin themes in the letter and, having just mentioned Christ's work, he now returns to God's Word. Some of his readers appear to have ignored and minimised the importance of biblical teaching (see 2:1). Only by the regular study of, and daily obedience to, the message of Scripture can Christians move from childish faith to spiritual maturity, from being helpless learners to helpful teachers (12,13).

How do we reconcile the slightly derogatory statement, 'for he is a child' (13; compare Eph. 4:14) with Paul's 'be imitators of God, as beloved children' (Eph. 5:1) and Peter's 'like newborn babes, long for the pure spiritual milk' (1 Pet. 2:2)? Is it not necessary to distinguish here between immature childishness and necessary child-like faith? Those who make the reading of God's Word part of their everyday lives also acquire necessary skills in discerning between what is good and what is harmful (14). But some of these first-century Christians never seem to have moved on from basic Christian truths to the more advanced aspects of the Christian message. In 6:1,2 our author describes six main topics in his course on 'Christian foundations'. These are certainly not to be disregarded, but he described them as 'elementary doctrines'; incidentally, they are aspects of faith which, in some measure, Christianity has in common with Judaism, an interesting point when one remembers this letter's first readers and their temptation to retreat back into their former 'Jewishness'. It is likely, however, that 'repentance from dead works' is a clear reference to one of Judaism's dangers (see Gal. 3:10; Eph. 2:8,9; Phil. 3:9; Heb. 9:9,10; 13:9) and a peril not confined to one religion but perilously characteristic of all. Even some Christians think they have to earn their salvation rather than receive it. The basic 'instruction about ablutions' (or 'baptisms') in the plural may refer to a necessary distinction between, say, the teaching of John the Baptist on the subject and that of the apostle Paul; such issues might well be a little bewildering to converts from Judaism.

THOUGHT: Note that at least one-third of these 'elementary doctrines' relate to the life to come (2b). Is that not sometimes a missing dimension in the teaching we give to young converts?

6:4–8 Thorns and thistles

Understandably, this passage has made the best of expositors tremble and, more seriously, has caused a number of sensitive Christians to be deeply disturbed. Unhappily, it has been linked in some people's thinking with the unpardonable sin (Matt. 12:31,32; Mark 3:28,29; 1 John 5:16,17) and, in a time of spiritual barrenness or disobedience, some believers have wondered whether they are among those who cannot be restored again to repentance (4). On this important subject, as with all other doctrines, it is essential to compare Scripture with Scripture. The Bible's *total* message is God's full revelation, not two or three verses taken completely out of their context and original setting.

Our author is not here describing some believer who carelessly allows his Christian life to drift, or a backslider who no longer gives meaningful expression to what seemed, at one time, a genuine and robust faith. The peril he feels compelled to expose is that of falling away from the living God (3:12), committing apostasy by holding 'up to contempt' the Christ they once loved (6). It is such a fierce form of Christ-rejection that it is starkly described as a renewed crucifixion. Those who are guilty of such rebellion totally disown their earlier allegiance to Christ and deliberately put themselves among the angry crowds on that first Good Friday, saying, 'Away with him. We will not have this man to reign over us.' People who persist in that kind of rejection cannot possibly be saved, for they despise the only person by whom salvation can be obtained. Some expositors have endeavoured to overcome the difficulty by suggesting that verses 4,5 describe an 'almost' or merely professing Christian, e.g. they only 'tasted' (5) the goodness of God's Word and did not actually receive it into their lives. But the same term is used in 2:9 to describe Christ's utterly real experience of death, not a merely fleeting contact with it, more apparent than real. The original context of this letter must be kept firmly in mind when one is seeking to interpret this passage (compare 10:26–31). One may justifiably ask whether any person guilty of this kind of hostile repudiation was ever genuinely 'born again'; such knowledge is reserved for God alone (2 Tim. 2:19). Such people forfeit the blessing of God (7,8); look up Deuteronomy 29:18–23 and Isaiah 5:1–7 for the Old Testament background to this agricultural illustration. It refers to the deliberate apostate and stubborn rebel, not the occasional backslider.

THOUGHT: F. F. Bruce is surely right when he says that 'continuance in the Christian life is the test of reality. The doctrine of the final perseverance of the saints has as its corollary the salutary teaching that the saints are the people who persevere to the end'.

6:9–12 Until the end

The writer of this letter is deeply persuaded that the hard things he has had to say about apostates do not apply to his readers (9). He is impressed by their loving service within the life of God's people (10). The omniscient God is certainly aware of our hidden motives and secret sins (4:13), but he does not overlook either our work for him or love for his children. The early seventeenth-century commentator, John Trapp, puts it rather beautifully: 'The butler may forget Joseph, and Joseph forget his father's house; but forgetfulness befalls not God, to whom all things are present, and before whom there is written a book of remembrance.' Notice that this service is not something which took place once or twice in the past; it is a continuing ('as you still do') expression of their gratitude to him. Although the doctrine of Christ's person and work is the central feature of this epistle, our author's understanding of God is not thereby forced into an insignificant background. With our understandable concentration on the Lord Jesus, are we not sometimes in danger of forgetting the Father?

In arresting language, this unashamedly Christocentric letter rightly reminds us that our Almighty Father is a speaking (1:1), gracious (2:9), living (3:12), all-knowing (4:13; 6:10), generous (6:13–15), reliable (6:18), welcoming (7:19), merciful (8:12), faithful (10:23), invisible (11:27), loving (12:6), just (12:23), holy (12:28,29) and mighty (13:20) God. All this surely encourages our 'sacrifice of praise' to him (13:15). Possibly some of the first readers of this letter were less committed to Christian service than others, for the author longs that 'each one' (11) of them will 'show the same earnestness' as those he commends. Christian life and work are inspired by hope (11) and motivated by faith, faith in a God who has made promises and always keeps his word. In his masterly exposition of this letter, Philip Hughes has reminded us that 'the Christian life must be marked by progress and perseverence *until the end* (compare Matt. 10:22; Mark 13:13; Rev. 2:26). Its direction is ever onward and upward (compare 12:1) and hope is one of its distinguishing characteristics – hope that is securely founded on the promise and the power of God and which itself is the dynamic impulse that drives us on toward the goal.'

THOUGHT: In this passage we are urged to be 'imitators' of those who have gone before (12). What kind of an example are we to those who are following closely behind? Notice the important place given to example in New Testament teaching, compare 1 Cor. 4:16; 11:1; Phil. 3:17; 4:9; 1 Thess. 1:6; 2:14; 2 Thess. 1:4 and especially John 13:12–15; Phil. 2:5; 1 Pet. 2:21.

6:13–20 Strong encouragement

Concerned lest some of his readers become 'sluggish' (12, the same word as 'dull' in 5:11), writer of this letter urges them to remember those who have persevered in difficult times by holding on to the promises of God. Abraham is the best possible Old Testament example of a man who, rich in faith, was sustained by hope. John Calvin says: 'Examples show us better things. If the bare doctrine is propounded it does not have the same effect as when we see what is demanded of us actually fulfilled in the person of Abraham. The example of Abraham is taken, not because it is unique, but because it is more outstanding than the others.' God made promises to Abraham (13,14; see Gen. 12:3,7; 13:16; 17:15,16; 22:15–18), but they were not fulfilled immediately. His faith in God was expressed in constantly renewed hope which is nothing other than faith on its tiptoes. Faith and hope of this character are not instantaneous blessings. We live in an age of 'instantly available' resources and sometimes imagine that the same thing can happen in our Christian lives. But some Christian qualities take a fair amount of time before they can be developed, strengthened, increased and used for the blessing of others. Abraham had to go through years of patient waiting (15) before he actually 'obtained the promise' and so became an example to us of steady endurance. How did Abraham go on believing and hoping when, humanly speaking, it seemed most unlikely that, with an ageing wife, the promise of a male heir would be fulfilled? Deep down in his heart Abraham was persuaded that *the promise of God* would not be broken. God would not say one thing today and then suddenly change his mind, withdrawing his earlier promise. Moreover, Abraham knew that to be true because of *the character of God*. The God of truth confirms the word of promise by the divine oath. These 'two unchangeable things' provide us with constant encouragement as we press on in hope, whatever the outward circumstances or occasional disappointments. But our hope ought to be stronger than Abraham's, for we have a source of encouragement he could not experience. As Christians we know that *the Son of God*, the Lord Jesus, has gone before us into heaven (19,20). He opens up the way and we follow in his steps.

THOUGHT: Commenting on this passage, John Brown reminds us that, as our 'forerunner', Jesus entered heaven 'on our account, for our advantage' and 'as our representative'. Those who have hope keep their eyes on Jesus.

Questions for further study and discussion on Hebrews 3:7–6:20

1. Can you think of practical ways in which, without becoming inquisitive busybodies in other people's affairs (see 1 Tim. 5:13), we can exercise a ministry of mutual exhortation (3:13), encouragement (10:24,25) and, where necessary, correction (12:15)?

2. Vincent Taylor has said that in this letter it is 'everywhere assumed' that sin 'constitutes a barrier to fellowship with God'. Make a study of our writer's doctrine of sin (e.g. 3:13; 11:25; 12:1,4), its nature, effects and consequences.

3. Does 4:9 refer to a procured, potential or ultimate 'rest'? What are the practical implications for everyday living?

4. How would you define the precise way in which the piercing action of the living and active sword of God's Word divides 'soul and spirit' and discerns the thoughts and intentions of our hearts?

5. How can we defend the conviction that Jesus has been tempted 'in every respect . . . as we are' (4:15) when we, by virtue of our life-style, encounter very different temptations, e.g. as married couples, women, elderly people, folk who live in a materialistic, technological society?

6. What can we learn from the writer's use of Old Testament Scripture? What guidelines are there for the place and interpretation of the Old Testament today?

7. How real is the danger of 'falling away'? Think of those you know who once professed faith but did not continue. What more could our churches and fellowships do to support and encourage new converts?

8. How would you assess the importance of the ascension? What are its practical consequences for the Christian life?

7:1–10 A Priest for ever

The extended passage about the need for spiritual maturity and confident endurance opened (5:10,11) and closed (6:20) with a reference to Melchizedek, a detail which the writer wanted to expand but felt he could not properly do so because many of his readers were 'dull of hearing'. He confesses that teaching of this kind is 'hard to explain' and only likely to be understood by those who are accustomed to 'solid food' (5:14). We have seen that our author rejoices in the Old Testament revelation of God's Word (1:1), and that he has already made effective reference to these Scriptures either to support, defend or illustrate his doctrinal convictions. His use of the Genesis 14:17–20 narrative follows naturally after his mention of Abraham (6:13) who was met by Melchizedek, the King of Salem (probably Jerusalem, see Ps. 76:2), after the patriarch's victory over some neighbouring pagan kings.

Melchizedek only makes one further appearance in the Old Testament, in Psalm 110:4, but he is a figure of great importance for our writer who argues as much from what Scripture does not say about him as from what it does. For example, the silence of Scripture on Melchizedek's ancestry and end becomes a significant foreshadowing both of Christ's eternal nature ('resembling' the pre-existent Son of God) and his unique work as 'a priest for ever' (3) who continues to exercise his ministry without end.

The names used in the Genesis narrative are also used in this vivid portraiture of Christ; Melchizedek = 'king of righteousness' and Salem = 'peace', both terms are rich in content not only as descriptive of Christ (Acts 3:14; 1 Cor. 1:30; Eph. 2:14–17; 1 John 2:1), but also of our salvation in him (Rom. 5:1,18; Phil. 1:11; 3:8,9; 4:7). But it is Melchizedek's greatness and superiority which is of the greatest importance to our writer here. He must have been greater than Abraham for the patriarch to have both needed and valued this king-priest's blessing; the 'inferior' person is always 'blessed by the superior'. When Abraham honoured Melchizedek by paying tithes to him, he was not only making a personal acknowledgment of his superiority; there was a sense in which at that moment all Abraham's progeny, including Levi, were 'in the loins of' (10) their great ancestor. In other words, Levi is also inferior to Melchizedek and the Levitical (or Aaronic) temporary priesthood is thereby inferior to Christ's eternal priesthood.

THOUGHT: 'Christ is greater than Melchizedek as the reality is greater than the facsimile. Therefore Christ is greater than Abraham, Levi, and all his descendants, and His priesthood too is greater than theirs' (G. F. Hawthorne). How foolish, therefore, for any first-century Jewish Christian to forsake Christ, thus turning from a superior to an inferior priesthood.

7:11–19 A better hope

In a variety of different ways this letter constantly asserts the supremacy of Christ over Jewish legalism and over any form of salvation by works or religious observances of one kind or another (9:9,10). Some of its first readers appear to have been tempted to retreat back into their earlier Judaism for, during times when Christians were fiercely persecuted by the Roman authorities, Jewish people enjoyed a measure of religious freedom and immunity from harassment and oppression. It was safe in the synagogue when it was dangerous in the church. But our author urges these Christian believers to recognise the Jewish priesthood and sacrificial system for what it was, an inspiring and highly evocative stage in the total revelation of God to his people, all brought to necessary fulfilment in the greater prophetic and unique priestly ministry of his redeeming Son. If the Aaronic priesthood exercised by Levi, his tribe and successors, had been perfectly adequate and eternally effective, then there would have been no need whatever for another priesthood. But such a radical change was necessary and God's appointed priest came not from the tribe of Levi but from Judah (11–14). Even the Melchizedek reference in the psalm he has quoted (17,21; see 5:6) anticipates the coming of an omnipotent and victorious Lord who, seated at God's right hand (Ps. 110:1,2), will exercise a priestly ministry which (in contrast to others) will last 'for ever' (Ps. 110:4).

The Old Testament itself looks beyond its own legalistic and sacrificial provisions to something 'better', a key word in this letter, see 7:19; 8:6; 9:23; 11:40. The Levitical priesthood could only be exercised by those who belonged to a particular family, but Christ's eternal priesthood is authenticated not by legal requirements of that character but by 'the power of an *indestructible* life'. It is a life which is impossible either to destroy or terminate. 'Other priests were made priests by virtue of a special ordinance: He was made priest in virtue of His inherent nature' (Westcott). The resurrection of the Lord Jesus clearly indicates that he is God's Son (Rom. 1:4), that his ministry cannot ever be dissolved and that it will remain eternally effective. The former sacrificial provisions have now been 'set aside'. They were an important stage in God's plan of salvation, constantly reminding man of his deep need (10:3) and pointing forward to a better sacrifice which would not only offer ceremonial cleansing necessary for acceptable worship, but the inward cleansing of our polluted and disturbed consciences (9:6–14).

THOUGHT: We need to remember that only the ceremonial law has been 'set aside because of its weakness and uselessness' (18). The moral law expounded in the Ten Commandments is as authoritative and relevant today as ever.

7:20–25 A permanent priesthood

It does not require a great deal of mental effort to realise how hard it was for first–century Jews to leave the synagogue for the local church. Our writer wants them to understand that all that is rich and permanent in the Old Testament tradition is still of abiding worth. The patriarchal narratives pointed forward to a coming priest-king (1–17), the Psalter is an important source for his teaching about Christ (17,21) and the prophets also anticipated a day when there would be a new covenant, far better than the old (8:6–13).

Eager to assert the permanence of Christ's priesthood, he explains that no Levitical priest was required to take an oath on the assumption of his office, but Christ's superior priestly ministry is authenticated not only by Christ's victorious resurrection, but also by God's dependable Word. If the Lord God has 'sworn' with an oath and has pledged that he 'will not change his mind' regarding the priesthood of Christ as a ministry which is 'for ever' (21), then surely they can trust what God has done (raising his Son from the dead, 13:20; Rom. 6:4; Col. 2:12) and what he has said (6:17,18; 10:23; compare Num. 23:19; 1 Sam. 15:29). As Christians, they must now look upon the Lord Jesus as 'surety', or as guarantor, of a far better covenant than the old one in which they participated as devout Jews. When this word 'surety' (*enguos*) appears in classical literature it describes someone who stands security and guarantees that some necessary legal obligation will be carried out.

Moreover, these priestly blessings bestowed by Christ as the only Redeemer (9:12) of God's people are not limited to his past achievement. Jesus exercises a *present* ministry as the believer's priestly intercessor. However devout he might be, death robbed every Old Testament priest of his ministry of prayer on behalf of the Israelite people. Once his heart stopped beating, compassionate intercessions were a thing of the past. But our eternal Priest ministers *for ever* (24). It is not only a permanent but also an effective priesthood. Those words which assert that Christ's ministry is 'for all time' (25) are important and have been variously translated as 'completely' (NIV) and 'absolutely' (NEB). The same phrase is used in a negative form in Luke 13:11, describing the crippled woman who could not *fully* straighten herself. It here describes Christ's limitless ministry and its complete adequacy.

THOUGHT: Believers can trust Jesus completely as their guarantor because of who he is, God's Son (7:3) and what he has achieved (9:14). Moreover, God himself authenticates Christ's unique work by his unfailing and completely trustworthy Word (5:5,6; 7:21).

7:26–28 Once for all

In his exposition of the closing section of this chapter, Philip Hughes quotes the words of an Italian commentator, P. Teodorico, who describes these verses as 'a hymn to the High Priest . . . as though an outburst of the joy of humanity which has at last found the High Priest qualified to understand its weaknesses and to come to its aid: so far above us and so near to us; himself in need of no cleansing and able to cleanse and expiate all our guilt'.

It is certainly true that Christ is here portrayed as one who, in his moral perfection, is 'so far above us'. We are sinful and bound to the things of this earth, but he is 'holy, blameless, unstained, separated from sinners, exalted above the heavens'. Every Old Testament priest was a sinner like every member of his local community, but Jesus was entirely sinless, a truth about his human life mentioned by more than one New Testament writer (2 Cor. 5:21; 1 Pet. 2:22; 1 John 3:5). There were no sins to mar his life. No atonement was necessary for him, as it was for the Levitical priests (27a). Because they too were sinners a *daily* sacrifice (possibly the sin offering which may well have been a daily necessity in any community, Lev. 4) atoned for their inadvertent (but not deliberate) sins. But Christ's unique sacrifice was offered 'once for all' (a key term in this letter) and not repeated daily. It was a divinely appointed and accepted atonement, and it was for rebellious sinners, not simply for the occasional, unwitting mistakes of priests (Lev. 4:3) and others.

Christ is also portrayed here as one who, in his spiritual vocation, is 'so near to us'. Because he has been tempted (2:17,18; 4:15), he knows how much we need the help which he alone can give. At immense cost to God (John 3:16), he came into this world as our redeemer. At incalculable personal cost, Christ 'offered up himself'. This was an entirely 'fitting' (26; compare 2:10), though totally undeserved, way of salvation; it is also completely dependable (confirmed by the divine oath) and continually effective (he saves us now, v. 25). Its reliability is emphasised again here (28) by the repetition of the 'oath' theme mentioned earlier in the letter. God's oath concerning the eternal priesthood of Christ (Ps. 110:4) superseded that law by which the Levitical priesthood was established.

THOUGHT: 'The power of his all-sufficient atoning work is available without diminishment to us today as it was to the believers of the first century, and it is so because he who died for us is alive from the dead and enthroned on high' (Philip Hughes).

8:1–7 A minister in the sanctuary

The closing verses of the previous chapter underline the sharp contrast found throughout this letter between the old and the new, the provisions of the Levitical priesthood and those of the high priestly ministry of the Lord Jesus. The Aaronic priesthood appointed men in their 'weakness', but God's Son is perfect; their ministry was terminated by death, but his lasts 'for ever' (7:28). Our gifted author presents a series of vivid contrast pictures in order to describe the 'better things' that are ours in Christ. Following the 'priesthood' theme (ch. 7), he now moves to consider the eternal sanctuary in heaven as opposed to the impermanent one on earth (8:1–5), and later, with equal artistry, portrays the new covenant as opposed to the old (8:6–9:14), and the *one* 'better' sacrifice of Christ in contrast with the *many*, and only partially effective, sacrifices under the law (9:23–10:18).

The Jewish Christian readers who first received this letter knew only too well that in Old Testament times the high priest ministered on behalf of the people in an earthly tent, a temporary sanctuary in the wilderness. But these things belong to Israel's past and the tabernacle was but a 'copy' or 'shadow' (5) of the heavenly sanctuary made by God. Some commentators are persuaded that our writer is here using Plato's concept of heavenly 'ideas' with earthly 'copies', but others insist that there is more dependence here on the Hebrew idea of promise and fulfilment than the teaching of Greek philosophers.

The important point here is that the sacrifice of Christ is eternally effective. It belongs not to the order of passing, impermanent things, but to the realm of eternal and unchanging realities which are for ever secure. With the aid of this arresting portraiture, these first-century believers are being urged once again to avoid slipping back into the impermanent, perishable realm of transient things. Their High Priest is in heaven, not on earth (1). The sanctuary where he ministers as their effective Advocate, eternal Saviour and compassionate Priest cannot be destroyed by invading armies (as the Jerusalem Temple had been). The Levitical priests had 'something to offer', either 'gifts' or 'sacrifices' (3). Jesus 'offered himself without blemish to God' (9:14). The priests did not personally bear the cost of these offerings unless they were to atone for their own sins; the cost was borne by the worshipper. But Christ's offering was *for us*, yet borne by him. His priestly ministry is 'much more excellent than the old' covenant. The fact that something new was necessary testifies to the 'weakness' (7:18) of the old (6,7).

THOUGHT: Christ our High Priest 'must have *had* something to offer' (NEB footnote rendering of 8:3). 'Love's redeeming work is done, Hallelujah!'

8:8–13 The better covenant

From the priesthood and its sanctuary our writer moves to one of the greatest themes of the Old Testament, the covenant. A covenant was an agreement made between two parties. It contained pledges and promises (6). The old covenant was a purely temporary measure and was not without faults (7), so in Jeremiah's time God, through the prophet, announced a new and better covenant that would eventually make the first 'obsolete' (13). The passage in Jeremiah 31:31–34 is important for our author who twice refers to it, here and in 10:16,17.

Note that the new covenant, with which God was determined to replace the old, was for *estranged* people; it would be for both Israel and Judah (8), the divided kingdom which had become marked by alienation and tension. Moreover, it was for *all* people (11), not just the houses of Israel and Judah; it would break through all manner of barriers and reach 'from the least of them to the greatest' (11). It was certainly for *sinful* people. Those who were brought out of Egypt by their Redeemer-God became disobedient rebels rather than grateful servants; they did not continue in God's agreement (9). In those days the law was external, written on stone, but they broke those laws within weeks of their initial promulgation (Exod. 20:4; 32:1–4). The new covenant would be written on the hearts of those who responded to his totally undeserved offer of generous, merciful forgiveness (12a). He promised (note the repetitive 'I will's in this great passage) to forget, as well as forgive, the sins of his people (12b). The old covenant is now obsolescent (13), though we need to take careful note here that our writer is saying that the *ceremonial* law has been abrogated, not the moral law. All men and women, Christian or otherwise, need God's moral law; the divine standards for personal conduct and corporate life in the Ten Commandments have never been withdrawn. Far from forsaking these, Christians accept even higher standards (Matt. 5:20–48). The former covenant, with its emphasis on outward, ceremonial purification, had now grown old; once Christ came it was destined to disappear (13b). Something far better has come, not external but inward, not restricted but universal, not uncertain but sure, not temporary but eternal.

THOUGHT: 'The words *I will be merciful toward their iniquities* show that the source of forgiveness is not human merit but God's mercy and grace. The ground of forgiveness is not man's repentance but the sacrifice of Christ' (Thomas Hewitt).

Questions for further study and discussion on Hebrews 7:1–8:13

1. Our author's use of the Melchizedek typology in chapter 7 would have made an immediate appeal to his Jewish Christian readers in the first century. Given proper safeguards, typological preaching and teaching can still be very effective, but what are its dangers?

2. If 'the law made nothing perfect' (7:19), what exactly was it meant to achieve? Does this mean that it can now be ignored?

3. Some of our contemporaries spend their lives in the vain pursuit of alternative forms of 'salvation'. Some are persuaded that this 'desire for a radical change' may be achieved by campaigning for political liberation, others by listening to the gurus of eastern mysticism, or by struggling for materialistic advancement, or by the self-absorbing quest for pleasure. What does our letter have to say about the uselessness (7:18) of these and other ways of obtaining an ideal and eternal life?

4. What practical difference does it make in our lives that Jesus 'always lives to make intercession' (7:25) for us, and is it possible for us to discern the precise character of his intercessory ministry (e.g. Luke 22:32; John 17:9,11,15–21; Rom. 8:34)?

5. In what respect is the new covenant better than the old?

6. What are the challenges to the superiority of Christ in our society? How do we meet them?

7. The tabernacle was full of symbols pointing to spiritual realities (9:1–5). What symbols are legitimate and helpful in our buildings and worship?

8. '. . . these first-century believers are being urged once again to avoid slipping back into the impermanent, perishable realm of transient things.' How does that temptation come today? How can it be met?

9:1–5 Holy things

With the discussion about the sanctuary (8:1–5) uppermost in his mind, our writer describes some of its features and furnishings. There are at least two points in this magnificent letter when the author rather tantalisingly says that he is not able to say more on a particular subject under review (9:5; 11:32a). How we wish, in both instances, he had not restricted himself to such a relatively brief 'word of exhortation' (13:22)! It would have been fascinating here to know what he would have said, had time and space permitted, about these various items. Would he have expounded their meaning typologically (as with Melchizedek), or explained their significance liturgically, or interpreted their message devotionally? We cannot know and it is pointless to speculate. John Calvin says that 'since nothing is enough for inquisitive men', our writer 'cuts out any opportunity for subtleties that are not in keeping with his present purpose in case too much discussion of these things might break the thread of his argument . . . There are some things which are not obscure and are suitable for the edification of faith; but we must show discretion and moderation in case we desire to know more than it has pleased God to reveal.'

What is of special interest to us is that, although our author knew that the old covenant was vanishing away (8:13), he did not lightly dismiss its sanctions, provisions and blessings. Far from it. He knows that some of his readers find it extremely difficult to abandon their Jewish beliefs and he is here telling them once again, yet in a different form, that they are not forsaking the best in their past, but witnessing its fulfilment. All its best dreams are realised in the coming of Christ. As Leon Morris has said, the writer of this letter 'clearly loved and had a profound interest in the Jewish institutions which foreshadowed the work of Christ. In a way without parallel in the New Testament, he dwells on the place and the manner of worship under the old covenant. Though now superseded, neither was without significance.' These items testified to God's holiness (2,3), faithfulness (4) and mercy (5), but these supreme qualities and values have been more perfectly manifested in God's Son, our holy (7:26), merciful and faithful (2:17) High Priest, man's Lord and Saviour, Jesus Christ.

THOUGHT: The riches of the tabernacle (4, note the threefold reference to gold) pale into insignificance when set alongside the incomparable wealth that is ours in Christ (2 Cor. 6:10; 8:9; Phil. 4:19).

9:6–10 Through the veil

With his detailed knowledge of Old Testament Scripture and his imaginative, Spirit-inspired interpretation of its truth, our writer now reminds these first-century Christians of the annual Day of Atonement (Lev. 16:1–34). Priests served in the outer court (6), but only the high priest was permitted to officiate in the Holy of Holies (3), and then only once a year (7), for this highly symbolic atonement festival. The writer is here at pains to emphasise that all this forcefully illustrates the necessity of something better. Moving and reassuring as the Day of Atonement was to the Hebrew people, it emphasised the limited and restricted nature of the provision which was made. The way was not open to all; even priests had to stay in the 'outer tent', let alone ordinary people. A way has to be provided for immediate access for *all* (compare 8:11,12). The Holy Spirit makes present use of this symbolic presentation of restricted access (8,9a) to show us that in Christ there is a 'new and living way' (10:19–21).

Moreover, it was not simply the fact that only the favoured few in the high priestly line could make this approach, but even when they went into the Holy of Holies, it was for a very limited form of cleansing. Their sacrifices provided ceremonial cleansing (10), but the man with a seriously wounded conscience was left unhelped (9). The ritual acts were highly important pictures, but they anticipated something far more radical and effective yet to come.

The Jewish Day of Atonement is vividly presented to these readers as 'an illustration for the present time' (9, NIV). It presented Old Testament worshippers with an unforgettably vivid portrait of the holiness of God, the importance of the law, the seriousness of sin, the necessity of cleansing, but the sensitive man or woman tormented by guilt and remorse was left with only limited help and a continuing sense of shame. 'But now Christ has come' (11, NEB) as our eternal, perfect and sinless High Priest. The Jewish high priests were privileged men, but were also sinners. They took the sacrificial blood to sprinkle on the mercy seat for their own sins as well as those of the congregation. But our greater High Priest, the Lord Jesus, offers his own blood (12) and not for his own sins (7:26), but for ours. How deeply grateful we ought to be that in Christ the 'time of reformation' has come.

THOUGHT: 'Not all the blood of beasts On Jewish altars slain, Could give the guilty conscience peace Or wash away the stain: But Christ, the heavenly Lamb, Takes all our guilt away; A sacrifice of nobler name, And richer blood than they.' (Isaac Watts)

9:11–17 How much more!

The high priest's work on the Day of Atonement did not reach into the depths of what John Bunyan described as 'the wounded conscience'. The annual Jewish ritual dealt with matters of external cleansing for ceremonial purposes. The sin offering made provision for anyone who sinned 'unwittingly' (Lev. 4:2), not the rebellious and deliberate offender who now wished to be different. The guilt offering (Lev. 5) was available for someone who had become defiled, for example, by touching something ceremonially 'unclean', but what of the troubled heart and mind of a remorseful sinner? Some 're-formation' (10) was surely necessary to meet the needs of sinful men and women through the centuries.

Thank God, these long-awaited 'good things' have now 'come' (11) in the perfect life, sacrificial death, authenticating resurrection and present intercession of Christ. We have now moved from God's temporary provision of the sacrificial system to something 'greater and more perfect' (11), God's eternal salvation procured by Christ. The constantly (and necessarily) repeated sacrifices of the ceremonial law are at an end; our great High Priest has entered 'once for all' into the presence of our holy God. He did not offer the blood of sacrificial animals, but his own blood (12). The sacrifice which he made for sinful mankind does not provide for occasional, ritual cleansing (13), but 'eternal redemption'. It does not simply purify the flesh so as to make the worshipper 'clean' from a ceremonial point of view. It reaches down into the defiled, profoundly disturbed, hidden depths of the human conscience. Moreover, it does not simply *cleanse* the conscience, glorious as that is, but it *liberates* the purified believer. Instead of focusing his introspective attention on the 'dead works' of the ceremonial law (or of his own self-righteousness, Phil. 3:9), the newly-released believer is made free to 'serve the living God' (14).

Eager to make his point unmistakably clear, our writer moves to a further illustration which takes his readers from the sphere of religious ceremonial to that of legal provision. He has already mentioned the concept of the *covenant* (8:6–9:1). This word *diathēkē*, 'testament', was also used to describe a will. Christ's death has made every Christian believer into an eternally grateful beneficiary. We have received 'the promised eternal inheritance' (15). The legacy could not have become ours until the benefactor died (16,17).

THOUGHT: Surely the fact that Christ has shed 'his own blood' (12) for us ought to remove our guilt, inspire our gratitude (14a, 'how much more') and motivate our service (14b). What a privilege it is to belong to 'those who are called' (15).

9:18–22 Costly forgiveness

By his brief but very telling reference to the legal illustration, the author of this letter has made it clear that the sacrificial death of Christ was a divine necessity. There was no other way by which 'the promised eternal inheritance' (15) could become ours. In a secularised society like our own, men and women are always exposed to the danger of alternative forms of 'salvation'. Man wants to redeem himself or effect his own salvation, radical change or improvement either by moral effort, or political liberation, or materialistic increase, or by pleasure-seeking escapism. With its frequent references to the Old Testament sacrificial system, this letter may seem far removed from the needs of late twentieth-century man. In point of fact its message has a startling relevance which exposes all man's futile attempts to build for himself a different kind of life or world order. It points to every individual's greatest need, inward cleansing and a power outside ourselves to make us into the people we, in our better moments, genuinely long to be. Even when men and women, by tireless effort and with commendable aims, have built a better society, it will still be composed of sinners who all have within themselves the most terrifyingly destructive potential. Degrading poverty, hunger, racial discrimination are certainly not part of God's purpose for mankind, but even if these godless things are removed, man cannot live harmoniously alongside his fellows. People may live in better homes, but marriage breakdown is an increasing heartache. To become right with God is man's greatest need and only then can he live harmoniously with his neighbours. The 'forgiveness of sins' (22) is the eternal priority and that could not be achieved without the shedding of Christ's blood. The Mosaic covenant was ratified in the presence of the people by the shedding and sprinkling of blood (19,20; Exod. 24:6–8) and the sacred vessels in the tabernacle and its furnishing were all marked by the sprinkled blood (21; Lev. 8:15,19; 16:14–16). In other words, the benefits of the sacrificial blood had to be applied in the lives of the people (Exod. 24:8). These verses remind us not only of the necessity and cost of our salvation, but also of its personal appropriation.

THOUGHT: The Lord's Supper reminds us that Jesus referred to 'my blood of the covenant, which is poured out for many for the forgiveness of sins' (Matt. 26:28). Accepting such costly pardon means that we must not hug our own sense of failure, as if our sins were unforgiven; and we dare not withhold our forgiveness from others, as if pardon were exclusively ours.

9:23–28 Full salvation

With a great gift for effective illustration, our writer has used a series of pictures and images, familiar to his readers, to portray the uniqueness of Christ's saving work. His priesthood is far superior to that familiar to Old Testament believers (7:1–28). The heavenly sanctuary is of far great significance than the tent in the wilderness (8:1–5). The new covenant is far more important and effective than the old (8:6–9:14). Believers in Christ have become the beneficiary legatees of an eternal inheritance (9:15–17), all made possible through the shedding of Christ's blood (9:18–23). He now moves to an exposition of Christ's essential death in terms of a saving sacrifice for mankind, contrasted once again with the temporary sacrificial system of the old covenant legislation.

The tabernacle and its furnishings, to which reference has just been made (18–22), was but an earthly copy of the heavenly reality; it was appropriate enough for these 'copies' to be cleansed by the blood of sacrficial animals, but if man's eternal salvation was to be procured, then it could only be by 'better sacrifices than these' (23).

Once more (as at 8:5) our author may be making use of the Platonic concept of 'ideas'. Some of his first readers may have been almost as familiar with Greek philosophy as Jewish religion and history. Plato suggested that earthly objects have a heavenly 'idea' or pattern and the author may have been using this particular illustration to drive a point home to readers with a Greek intellectual background. The heavenly sanctuary is the eternal one; the earthly tabernacle was but a copy (24) or a replica of that heavenly one where Christ has entered. Even the Jewish high priest, with all his privileges, could not enter into the Holy of Holies on ordinary days; only on one day in the year could atonement be made there. But our great High Priest has entered into the presence of the eternal God (24) for us. He does not present animal blood, but his own (25). He does not offer it repeatedly, but once (26). He does not procure a purely ceremonial cleansing, but the removal of human sin. It is 'put away', or done away with (NIV), by his own unique sacrifice (26).

QUESTION: When Jesus comes again it will not be to deal with sin (as at his first coming), but to complete his saving work in the lives of all those 'who are eagerly waiting for him' (27,28). How can our eagerness for Christ's return be given practical expression?

10:1–10 'Thy will' – nothing less

More than once in this magnificent letter its author has insisted that the Old Testament ceremonial law could only meet a fragment of man's moral and spiritual need. It could offer the covenant community a necessary awareness of God's holy nature and his moral demands; it emphasised the need for external purity when approaching him in worship and it naturally made its adherents more sensitive to the blight of sin and its corruptive influence in human life. But the law's cultic provisions (9:9,10) did not meet the need of a heart-religion. The ceremonial law was a 'shadow of the good things to come' (1; compare 9:11) and with the coming of Christ these 'good things' have not only come but are here to stay. How foolish then to go back to merely external and purely temporary provisions, forsaking Christianity by returning to Judaism. These ceremonial obligations were not only a temporary 'shadow'; they were always unfinished and inevitably incomplete. More than that, they were only partially effective. They could not meet the deep, inward needs of those many guilty people who looked to God for his total cleansing and assured pardon (1,2). Their greatest value was primarily in their corrective influence; they served as a constant reminder of man's sinfulness. 'Year after year' (3) may be reminding us once more of the annual Day of Atonement (Lev. 16), but ritual of that or any other kind could not 'take away sins' (4). Only the sinless and obedient Redeemer could do that by the offering of himself. Psalm 40:6–8 is quoted at this point; even in Old Testament times God made it clear to his people that there was something of far greater value to him than sacrificial ritual, religious ceremony or correct liturgy – an obedient heart and a surrendered body (5–8). The psalmist recognises that the sacrifices offered by the Jewish people were not specially desired by God (5) nor were they particularly pleasing to him (8). This appears puzzling in view of the fact that God instituted the sacrificial system, but what is meant here is that they are utterly useless in themselves if they are not outward symbols of man's inner contrition, obedience, love, dependence and loyalty. 'Their value was in what they represented' (B. F. Westcott).

THOUGHT: Merely to present a costly offering was worthless if the outward worshipper was an inward rebel. But even if he is utterly sincere, man's best sacrifice cannot atone for his sin. Only the perfect offering of 'the body of Jesus Christ' (10) can effect our redemption.
Sealed my pardon with His blood:
Hallelujah! What a Saviour!

10:11–18 We are being sanctified

Christ's sacrifice is unrepeatable, complete and effective. The posture of the devout Old Testament priest emphasised the repetitive nature of the sacrificial system. He *stood* as the sacrifices were offered, but our great High Priest *'sat down* at the right hand of God' (11,12). The best sacrifice, lovingly offered under the old covenant, made the devout worshipper ceremonially clean and his worship acceptable, but it was not designed to remove for ever the worshipper's transgression (11), nor give him that assurance of complete pardon for which many must have longed. In Old Testament times the priests and holy vessels were 'sanctified' or 'set apart' for God's use; under the provisions of the new covenant the *worshipper* is sanctified through the unique offering of Christ's sinless body on the cross. In this letter's teaching, sanctification is both an accomplished fact (10, 'we have been sanctified') and a continuing process (14, NIV, we are 'being made holy'). It is effected by the work of Christ and the Word of God (15–17). Without the teaching of this Word, originally inspired by the Spirit's influence (2 Peter 1:21) and constantly brought to our remembrance by his present work (John 14:26; 16:13; 1 Cor. 2:6–13), no man or woman can possibly be sanctified.

The 'new covenant' teaching of Jeremiah 31 is here mentioned again (see 8:8–12), with its rich testimony to the inwardness of the law written on our hearts and not simply expressed in outward ritual (16), and the assurance of eternal forgiveness (17,18), based on the unfailing promise of a faithful God, not on the repeated sacrifices of devout men. These verses address themselves directly to late twentieth-century pluralistic society with its many religions, and their devoted adherents in our own neighbourhoods. The repeated offerings of the Jewish priest (11) typify the repetitive ritual of many world religions. Their teachings may present some fragment of truth about man, morality, love, neighbourliness, but the New Testament insists that all this 'can never take away sins'. As Christians, we must listen, carefully and respectfully, to what devout adherents of other religions are saying to us, show them our faith by genuine love as well as by verbal conviction, and acknowledge that not all that has gone by the name of 'Christian' has been worthy of the name. But we must always remain loyal to the biblical testimony that only in Christ can man be saved (John 14:6; Acts 4:12).

REMEMBER: In a religiously pluralistic society an apostle reminded his young colleague of this great fact: 'There is one God, and there is one mediator between God and men, the man Christ Jesus, who gave himself as a ransom for all' (1 Tim. 2:5,6a).

10:19–25 Hearts sprinkled clean

The main central section of the letter has focused the reader's attention on the uniqueness of Christ's work as totally transcending the Jewish sacrificial system, just as its opening section directed the mind to the uniqueness of his person as infinitely superior to the angels. The exposition of the person of Christ in the earlier chapters in the letter invites the reader to 'draw near' to the one who has also been tempted (4:14–16) and the central section closes with a similar application, though here the exhortation is widened to include corporate responsibility (24,25) as well as personal access (22) and individual loyalty (23).

The earlier chapters have emphasised the purity and holiness of a God who could not be approached intimately and directly except by one man (the high priest). The heavy curtain which separated the Holy of Holies from the Holy Place in the earthly sanctuary (9:1–3) kept even the most devoted worshipper at a distance (9:8). With his love of symbolism, our author reminds his readers that when the heavy dividing curtain (6:19) was torn on that first Good Friday (Matt. 27:51), it was but an outward material expression of a more costly and significant cleavage. On that day the far more important divided 'curtain' was the perfect body of the Lord Jesus, cruelly torn and broken for us. Since then every believer has immediate access. It is not restricted to the Jewish high priest once a year; it is now open for everyone who believes. We have a far better Priest, 'a great Priest', who rules over God's house, the church (21), and at his invitation we follow him into the sanctuary where he has gone ahead of us (6:20; compare 2:10). We approach him with sincerity ('a true heart', compare Matt. 5:8), confidence ('in full assurance of faith', compare 4:16), and purity ('hearts sprinkled clean . . . and our bodies washed', compare Ezek. 36:25).

It may seem strange to us that, having emphasised the superiority of heart religion to external ceremony, our writer now links the sprinkled heart with a washed body. But baptism, which may be intended here, was an outward symbol of the inward reality (see 1 Pet. 3:21, NEB). Consistent and unwavering witness (23) is also important for those who belong to 'the house of God', and a faithful God will keep his promise to uphold those who speak for him (1 Cor. 1:5–9; 10:13; compare Luke 21:12–19).

THOUGHT: Remember that the mutual encouragement of other believers is just as important as persuasive testimony to outsiders (24,25; compare 1 Thess. 5:11). The promised return of Christ ought to inspire both evangelism and fellowship. Neglecting the Christian meeting (25a) minimises our witness in society, impoverishes the corporate life of God's people, and hinders our spiritual development.

Questions for further study and discussion on Hebrews 9:1–10:25

1. Bearing in mind such references as Luke 24:27; Romans 15:4; 1 Corinthians 10:6,11, how would you begin to 'speak in detail' about the furnishings of the 'earthly sanctuary' mentioned in 9:1–5?

2. The author of Hebrews believes that the death of Christ has a profound effect on the human 'conscience'. Does his teaching about a purified conscience in 9:14 (also 9:9) indicate anything more than the assurance of forgiveness?

3. If the Old Testament sacrifices could not give 'inward perfection' (9:9, NEB; compare 10:1) or complete cleansing (10:2,3), what was their precise function in the life of a devout Jewish believer?

4. If, through the perfect sacrifice of Christ, 'we have been sanctified (10:10, an accomplished act), by what necessary processes are we *being* made holy' (10:14, NIV, a continuing action as in 2:11)? There is a similar emphasis in the New Testament between salvation as both an accomplished and a continuing work. What do we learn from this?

5. By what practical means can Christian believers 'stir up one another to love and good works' (10:24)?

6. How would you explain to a new Christian the importance of meeting together (10:25)? Why do you think some Christians seem to be so reluctant to gather together?

7. What do you see as the significance for the Jewish worshipper of the Day of Atonement? Are there elements that should still be part of Christian worship?

8. The writer of Hebrews could call on a common fund of Old Testament knowledge and experience to explain and illustrate 'the way of salvation'. How can we explain it to our contemporaries with no background knowledge of the Bible or Christianity?

10:26–31 I am the door

The preceding verses have exhorted these first-century believers to exercise the ministry of mutual encouragement, especially in the light of absenteeism (25). But what of those professing Christians who, because of the pressures of threatened or actual persecution from their fellow Jews in the synagogue, refuse to return to the local church? Even 'after receiving the knowledge of the truth' (26) of Christ's unique person and work, they insist on abandoning their former Christian testimony, preferring to become what they were before, Jewish believers enjoying the political protection and social privileges of the synagogue. In other words, they deliberately take their stand with those who totally reject the salvation which is found in Christ alone. They become numbered with those who regard Christ as a blasphemer or impostor (Matt. 26:65,66; 27:29,40–43), not man's only Saviour. How can anybody be saved if they insist on vehemently denying the only way by which salvation can be obtained? Surely for such people 'there no longer remains a sacrifice for sins' (26), and only judgment remains (27).

Our author here makes skilful use of the 'how much more' argument (28,29) he used at the beginning of the letter (2:2,3). Note that this deliberate act of rejecting Christ involves, in effect, a rejection of all three persons of the Trinity. Christ's deity is spurned and his sacrificial death despised (29), the gracious Holy Spirit, who brings initial enlightenment and continuing instruction, is 'outraged' (29b; compare Eph. 4:30), and the living God's wrath is aroused (30,31).

These verses are obviously not describing the believer guilty of some spiritual or moral lapse, nor the careless or even stubborn backslider. They portray one of the deliberately Christ-rejecting Jews of the first century whose earlier Christian profession has now become anathema to them. Surely anyone who takes up such an attitude of fierce hostility to Christ (profaning the blood of the covenant) can hardly have been 'born again' by God's Spirit in the first place. Perseverance and endurance are proof of a genuine conversion experience. The New Testament hardly encourages the view that, in some remote transactional sense, any man or woman who makes a profession of faith in Christ is thereby automatically saved whatever the character of their subsequent lives. The Saviour who taught that his sheep will never perish also said that they follow him (John 10:27–29) and that they can be recognised by the 'fruits' of consistent living (Matt. 7:20).

THOUGHT: 'The apostate must perish, not because the sacrifice of Christ is not of efficacy enough to expiate even his guilt, but because, continuing in his apostasy, he will have nothing to do with that sacrifice which is the only available sacrifice for sin' (John Brown).

10:32–39 The best is yet to be

We have no grounds whatever for assuming that the apostates described in the preceding verses were found in any significant numbers. Indeed, some have cogently argued that they may not even have existed and that our author is simply describing the serious eternal consequences of deliberate Christ-rejection, even in the life of one who made some earlier confession of faith. It is hard to believe, however, in the light of such strong expressions, that at some point or other the church to which this letter was originally addressed had not been wounded by the sin of apostasy. Here its author urges his readers not to look to the apostates, real or imaginary, but to the heroes; not to the rejectors, but to the martyrs and courageous witnesses of former days.

Probably this church's greatest problem is lethargy rather than apostasy. They need persistence and endurance (35,36) of the kind their forefathers had, or even that which many of them personally displayed in an earlier persecution when church members were publicly abused (33) or imprisoned, their homes plundered and personal possessions destroyed or removed (34a). In such times of adversity believers are urged to remember their assured future (34b–36) and to deliberately recall the promises and warnings of God's Word (37,38). They might lose their earthly possessions, but their heavenly possession is a 'better' and 'an abiding one' (34). The wealth which lies before them far exceeds the value of their most treasured possessions (see 2 Cor. 4:17,18; 1 Pet. 1:4–7). In this forward march toward that indestructible future, these pilgrims must remember what God has clearly said in the past. The one who has made promises is true to his word (23b; 11:11). They will 'receive what is promised' (36) if they believe what is said (37–39).

Our writer once again draws on the rich teaching of Old Testament Scripture and turns, appropriately enough, to Habakkuk, who preached in extremely tough times.

In those days of great stress, God's loyal but bewildered people were clearly told that the Lord's promises would be fulfilled (Hab. 2:3); the summons is to continuing faithfulness (Hab. 2:3,4). It was a most apposite word for these Jewish Christians under threat of renewed persecution. Those who are truly Christ's redeemed people will not 'shrink back' (39), but will press on like those valiant believers who were encouraged by Habakkuk's ministry in the late seventeenth century BC (Hab. 3:17–19).

THOUGHT: The reference to these courageous Old Testament 'saints' (37,38) introduces the most detailed exposition of faithful heroism to be found in early Christian literature (11:1–40). Remember that Jesus told his men that in persecution they should remember those who had gone before, as well as the glory yet to be (Matt. 5:11,12).

11:1–7 The faith-creating word

We have come to what is probably the most familiar section of the letter, but remember that, although this chapter is often considered in isolation, it builds on what has gone before. John Calvin made that clear when he said that 'whoever made this the beginning of the eleventh chapter broke up the sequence wrongly. The purpose of the apostle is to support what he has said . . . we shall never arrive at the goal of salvation unless we are furnished with patience.' Faith is necessary for the Christian journey to the better things that are promised, and faith is not some artificially induced buoyancy or pious but groundless hope. It is confidence in what God has said and done. Faith is accepting that what the Lord has declared is true. It is a testimony not to our loyalty but his integrity. For the man or woman of faith the future is as real and sure as the present. The word 'assurance' (1) is found in Greek papyri to describe a guarantee. As William Manson has said, faith is here expounded as 'a firm assurance with regard to the objects of our hope'. The Old Testament believers knew that there were far better things in store for them. That did not mean that they were like escapist ostriches who buried their heads in the sand. Faith did not simply enable them to look forward; it provided them with the resources to make a proper evaluation of the things around them. To quote William Manson again, faith convinced them about 'the reality of the invisible world'. They refused to accept things purely at their face value.

Faith of this character meets with God's approval (2). It relies on the powerful, unfailing word of a God whose promises are not only sure but effective. At creation, God said it, and it was done (3; Gen. 1:3,6,9,14,20,24). Abel (4) and Enoch (5) are among the earliest examples of those who 'received divine approval'. The 'more acceptable sacrifice' than that offered by Cain was that which involved the shedding of blood (9:22). Noah is a near perfect example of one who was given 'the assurance' (1) of things 'unseen' (7); that assurance brought salvation to his own household, condemnation to an unbelieving society and became, to subsequent generations, a testimony of obedience ('took heed', compare 2:1) and trust.

THOUGHT: Those things that are 'not seen' (1) are the eternal and abiding things (2 Cor. 4:18). Faith of this kind enabled Moses, for example, to look not at the proverbial treasures of Egypt, but at the eternal reward promised by God (11:26); he had a vision for invisible as well as merely visible things.

11:8–12 Abraham's venture

Understandably enough in a letter written to Jewish Christians, the faith of Abraham, the father of the race (8,12, 17–20), and Moses, the giver of the law (23–29), is given the greatest prominence. Abraham's faith is of rich exemplary value, for he too had 'the assurance of things hoped for' (1), 'received divine approval' (2) and put his confidence in the word which was powerful enough to create something new (3) out of a situation which seemed dead and hopeless. It was, moreover, not a static faith, but a confidence which lured him on and led him out. Accepting God's truth, he pressed on to the promised inheritance. During the day, the desert sand beneath his feet (he was 'living in tents' rather than resting on the firm foundations of a secure city, see 10,16; 12:22; 13:14) and the vast galaxy of stars at night became a visible testimony to the dependable promises of God (12). These everyday things reminded him of what God had clearly said (Gen. 13:16; 15:5,6; 22:17) and with that confidence he could march on when, from a purely human point of view, the situation was becoming increasingly desperate. He was getting older and so was his wife. She was now well beyond the normal age for childbearing (11), but for all that she conceived. The detail that she was 'past the age' (11) and he was 'as dead' (12) underline the wonder of the miracle, the incomparable might of God, and the reliability of the word he had revealed. In his exposition of this passage, Calvin reminds us of the primacy of the word. Abraham 'did nothing that was not by the command of God. This is surely one of the principles of faith that we do not move a step unless the word of God shows us the way and shines before us like a lantern.'

The faith of the patriarch involved him in costly sacrifice. He was called to forsake his home (Gen. 12), some of his treasured possessions (compare 10:32–34), and many of those he loved. What 'he was to receive' (8) was of greater importance than what he had left. The summons to Abraham to leave 'kindred', mentioned particularly by Stephen (Acts 7:3), may be an invitation to Christians to face the cost of social isolation as believers in time of persecution.

THOUGHT: Some may have been tempted to return to the synagogue, a safer place than the local church. But Christians have to be prepared to go out from securities of that kind, just as Jesus had to go out beyond the confines of Judaism (Heb. 13:12–14). We must be prepared to follow him, if necessary to the place of opposition, isolation and even rejection.

11:13–16 God's own people

Patriarchal faith is the main subject expounded in the next section of this inspiring chapter. Isaac and Jacob (9) were 'heirs' with Abraham of the same reliable promises. Our writer looks away from the outstanding individual, Abraham, to a greater company: 'These *all* died in faith' (13). Not all who exercise true and exemplary faith become famous. Thank God for the anonymous faithful multitude, people whose names will scarcely find their way into a church history textbook, but whose lives have meant more to us than many of those names who have. The lives of those believers who lived in the patriarchal period were clearly marked by certain commendable characteristics. They 'greeted' the future things 'from afar'; they hailed these future blessings at a distance and recognised that one day they would inherit what was promised. They had a faith which could anticipate blessings as well as appropriate them.

We live in an 'instant' age; everything must be done promptly, speedily or immediately and, unhappily, something of that spirit can invade our understanding of Christian experience. Some are seeking instant power, whilst others want instant sanctity or instant success. But patient waiting appears to have been an essential ingredient in early church life (Acts 1:4). How could we possibly acquire Christian virtues and qualities, such as longsuffering and patience, if we had everything we wanted and at the moment we wanted it? Paul believed that we need special power for the exercise and development of steady patience (Col. 1:11). These patriarchal heroes and heroines 'did not receive what was promised' (39), but their patient endurance produced in them a faith which was rich and strong.

Such people did not only press on; they spoke about the things they had 'seen' (13,27). They made open confession of their attitude to this passing world. They were aliens and exiles (13b; see 1 Pet. 2:11,12), making their way to a 'better country' (16). Their goal was not the increase of material possessions, or social status, or economic security; they focused their gaze on an imperishable 'homeland' (14). The 'land from which they had gone out' (15, is that a gentle aside directed at those tempted to return to the safety of the synagogue?) was behind them. They moved steadily on, not to the crumbling city which they had left, but to the secure one which God had prepared (16).

THOUGHT: Their Jewish or pagan neighbours may well have been ashamed of these believers, but their God was certainly not ashamed. Happy to be known as 'their God', he took pride in them. They are his treasured possession, 'a people claimed by God for his own' (1 Pet. 2:9, NEB).

11:17–23 The faith of old and young

Abraham believed so passionately in what God had said (17,18) that even though the Lord seemed to be going back (Gen. 22:2) on an earlier promise (Gen. 17:19–21; 21:1), the patriarch was convinced that God would keep his word, even if it meant raising Isaac from the dead (19). The narrative makes it clear that Abraham really did expect to come back down the mountain–side with his son (Gen. 22:5). If God had not provided a lamb, then he would have perfomed a resurrection. He would certainly not have gone back on his word.

This important emphasis on the dependability of the divine word naturally affected the Hebrew understanding of human speech too; once a word, say of blessing, was spoken, it could not be withdrawn. Isaac 'invoked future blessings' on Jacob and Esau; the children are mentioned not in order of birth but of privilege. Isaac, Jacob and Joseph are mentioned together here as those who, in the face of death (Gen. 27:1–4), could speak confidently about the future. At the end of their days (21,22) their faith remained strong and undiminished. They would not live to see the promised blessings on earth, but there were greater glories yet to be. Death was not the end of such believers.

For Isaac, as for the others mentioned here, 'death was but a mile-stone along the way to that "better country" on which his hope was fixed' (Philip Hughes). Jacob blessed Joseph's sons (21), anticipating future blessings (Gen. 48:8–20), and told Joseph that he would be brought to the promised land (Gen. 48:21). Joseph so believed in the truth of that word that, as an act of faith, he made provision for his coffin to be carried to Canaan (22; Gen. 50:25,26; Exod. 13:19; Josh. 24:32).

There were dark days and many bitter experiences for the Hebrew people between the death of Joseph and the birth of Moses. From the faith of dying men our writer moves to the faith of younger people. Although the Egyptian authorities had ordered the execution of all Jewish male children, Moses' parents 'were not afraid of the king's edict' (23). The faith of the frail and elderly Isaac, Jacob and Joseph, verbally expressed in their dying blessings, is deliberately followed by a reference to the heroism of young parents. They, too, long that the future promised blessings might be inherited at least by their children if not by themselves.

THOUGHT: When hiding became impossible, the faith of Moses' parents had a practical dimension. They were enabled to think out a way of deliverance for their baby just as, years later, Moses himself was used to execute, with equally careful attention to detail, a greater deliverance for God's people.

11:24–31 Faith laughs at impossibilities

The story of Moses, the exodus and the entry into Canaan naturally provided a series of brilliant illustrations of the kind of faith necessary for these first-century Christians in time of danger. The faith of Moses was such that he could clearly discern between things of merely temporary and transient significance and the greater things which lay beyond. He was enabled, by faith alone, to make deliberate and costly choices. Moses had social honours (24), the prospect of increasing physical satisfaction (25) and monetary wealth, but his faith was such that he was enabled to look away from all that to the promised reward (26). 'Ill-treatment with the people of God' (25), 'abuse suffered for the Christ' (26) and 'the anger of the king' (27) were not harsh experiences locked away in the distant past. Some of this letter's first readers had suffered in this way (10:32–34) and, as the years went by, the persecution of Christians by the secular authorities was going to be far worse than that inflicted upon them by hostile Jewish neighbours. These first–century believers needed a faith as strong as that of Moses at the exodus. He did not look at Pharaoh's angry countenance, nor the fearful faces of his contemporaries, or (later) the fierce faces of the pursuing armies, nor the bewildered faces of his terror-stricken compatriots. He looked up to the face of the God who could not be seen.

The portraiture of God in this chapter is worthy of special study. He is powerful (3), generous (6), just (7), dependable (10), faithful (11), loving (16), sovereign (19) and invisible (27). It is possible that, at a time when many believers, deeply committed to *Christ*, have rightly discovered a renewed interest in the work of the *Holy Spirit*, the doctrine of God, 'the forgotten *Father*', needs reappraisal. The faith of Moses was not only courageous; it was marked by the quality of obedience. He did what God said. He 'kept the Passover and sprinkled the blood' (28; compare 12:24; 9:22). Victorious faith like that of the godly who left Egypt (29) and those who entered Canaan (30) is, once again, a trust in what God has promised to do. Even an immoral Gentile foreigner can be saved if she obeys (31; 5:9). Those who believe prove that there are no limits to his mercy.

THOUGHT: Like his unafraid parents (23b), Moses endured, 'not being afraid' (27a). He reflected not only on what he had heard from his parents, but also on the rich faith exemplified in their lives. What kind of faith are we showing to our children, family, friends, neighbours and colleagues at work?

11:32–40 Well attested by their faith

This passage begins with one of the most tantalising verses in this attractive letter. Whatever would our author have said, had he enough time, about such judges, kings and prophets as Gideon, Barak, Samson, Jephthah, David and Samuel? These people were far from perfect. Fearful Gideon, crippled by a ghastly inferiority complex (Judg. 6:15), is followed here by insecure Barak, who will only go to war if that strong woman, Deborah, is at his side (Judg. 4:4–10,14). Samson may seem a surprising choice in view of his appalling mistakes, and he is certainly an encouraging reminder to every reader of this passage that things are never too bad for God (Judg. 16:22,28–30). And Jephthah? Understandably, Calvin asks, 'who would not at first have condemned the deed of Jephthah as rashness (Judg. 11:30–40) when he professed that he would be the avenger of his people when they were already hopeless?' For all his mighty achievements and uplifting songs, David was not always a model of good deeds (2 Sam. 11; Ps. 51), and Samuel was better at prophecy than parenthood (1 Sam. 8:1–3). John Calvin was surely right when he said: 'In every saint there is always to be found something reprehensible . . . There is no reason, therefore, why the fault from which we labour should break us or discourage us provided we go on by faith in the race of our calling.'

The faith of that vast anonymous multitude, which no man can number, is then described in outline and it is pointless to try to identify each of these people from the qualities characteristic of them. Many virtues have more than one claimant anyway. The anonymity is deliberate and ought to be preserved. It is telling us in unmistakable terms that faith is not just for the great characters of Old and New Testaments, but for us also. If we depend utterly upon the God who has spoken and acted in Christ, it will be faith with both active and passive characteristics. It will offer, and assure us of, the power to do difficult things (33–35a) and, possibly even more important, it will provide us with the resources to put up with things we cannot change (35b–38). These Old Testament believers pressed forward with outstretched hands to what was always on the horizon of their difficult lives. Although in one sense they 'received promises' (33), they could not 'receive what was promised'. Their rich faith awaited its fulfilment in the future when Christ would come.

THOUGHT: Like ourselves, these people could 'not be made perfect' without Jesus. Only through his work could they be brought to glory (2:10). Knowing he is at our side, ought we not to have an even better testimony than theirs?

Questions for further study and discussion on Hebrews 10:26–11:40

1. Suppose a person guilty of the serious apostasy described in 10:26–31 came later to regret such violent opposition to Christ; what, in your view, would the rest of Scripture have to say to such a person?

2. Passive endurance of suffering is one thing, but joyful acceptance is another (10:34). How can one *rejoice* in suffering as New Testament believers were certainly encouraged to do (Matt. 5:11,12; Rom. 5:3; Jas. 1:2; 1 Pet. 4:13)?

3. Calvin maintained that believing that God 'exists' (11:6) means keeping him continually in mind in all that we do: 'unless the Lord holds us to a firm knowledge of himself all kinds of doubts creep in to crowd out every sense of divinity. The human intellect is particularly prone to this kind of vanity so that it is easy to forget God.' In all the pressures and demands of a busy life, how can one cultivate this sense of God's existence and presence?

4. How does one maintain the attitude of being 'strangers and exiles' (11:13) in a society which lives as though this world is everything? Does the teaching of Hebrews 11 say anything to us about a distinctively Christian life-style and a concern for the world's poor?

5. What particular event was in the mind of our author when he wrote that Moses 'left Egypt' (11:27)? Was it the exodus, and if so, is it not strange to put that before (rather than after) the Passover reference (11:28)? Or was it the earlier flight of Moses from Egypt into Midian (Exod. 2:14,15)? The anger of Pharaoh was certainly a factor in both events and on each occasion 'faith' accomplished different things for Moses. What things?

6. 'If only you had more faith. . .' What does Hebrews 11 say to those Christians who seem to believe that a greater measure of faith would ensure that everything would happen as they wished?

7. If you are in a study group, each choose the character from Hebrews 11 with whom you most readily identify. Share your reasons and what you learn from that character.

8. Could you write a modern version of Hebrews 11? What characters from recent history, or from the present, are the greatest encouragement to you?

12:1–3 The unfinished race

Surrounded as we are by the vast company of those who have already run the race, we too press on to the goal. Many of the Old Testament believers the author has mentioned found their race extraordinarily difficult; it was impossible to avoid suffering. Look back at the chapter and see how true that is of most of the individuals mentioned by name and all of the anonymous multitude in the verses which close the previous chapter. But all their hardship and adversity cannot be compared with the sufferings of Christ. To look *at* their lives will bring challenge, warning, rebuke and inspiration, but to look *to* him will provide us with resources for the race. Christian believers are 'not of those who shrink back' (10:39); they 'run with perseverance' (same word as 'endurance' 10:36). To run effectively, the athlete must get rid of surplus 'weight' of any kind, physical or material; our progress is hindered if our lives become entangled by 'sin'.

The exhortation to 'look' employs a word used to describe someone who, though aware of other places where he might look, deliberately chooses not to direct his gaze anywhere else. Our eyes, like theirs, must be 'fixed on Jesus' (NEB), who has already been described by our writer as one who fully understands us; the human name of *Jesus* (2) is often used in this letter to heighten that sense of his compassionate and sympathetic identification with our human experience (see 2:9; 4:14,15; 5:7; 6:20; 13:12). As our pioneer, path-finder or trail-blazer, he goes on before us, just as, exercising his ministry as the pre-incarnate Christ, he went on ahead of all those Old Testament contestants. He is, moreover, not only the one who initiated our faith, but he brings it to completion. Some of these first readers may have been tempted to think that although they began the race by following their pioneer, they could only continue it by reliance on ceremonial works or moral effort. But Christ is the one 'on whom faith depends from start to finish' (2, NEB). The way to 'the throne of God' was not easy for the Son of God, but he too 'endured'. Those who constantly 'consider him' (3; compare 3:1) are not likely to drop out of the race, lacking the necessary strength.

THOUGHT: The writer of Hebrews does not address this congregation as a detached observer, content merely to point out their failures and shortcomings. He identifies closely with them as a skilful pastor: 'Let us . . . let us' (1; see 2:1; 4:11,16; 6:1; 10:22–25; 12:28; 13:13,15). He needs to look to Jesus as much as they do. Good teachers remain eager learners.

12:4–11 The Father's correction

How easily and skilfully our author moves through the pages of the Old Testament as he searches for the most appropriate quotation to make his point to Jewish Christian readers. Prophecy (8:8–12; 10:16,17,37,38) and psalmody (10:5–7), ceremonial legislation (9:1–10) and inspiring narratives (11:1–38), are now joined by proverbial sayings (5,6; Prov. 3:11,12). Those whose distinctively Christian faith is wavering and who do not want to lose all that is best in Judaism will surely feel encouraged that, in the development of their Christian experience, the Old Testament and its teaching will continue to play a most important part. Though there is no longer any place for sacrifices and other cultic regulations, that does not mean for a moment that everything they knew and loved as Jews had been left behind; far from it. Some of their treasured sayings, like those in Proverbs, will continue to enrich their minds and direct their wills to higher things.

Some of the first readers of this letter had known and experienced suffering; loyalty to Christ had brought some of them to prison (10:32–34; 13:3), but none of them to death (4). There is a necessary 'struggle'; the athletic imagery is widened here by the use of a boxing term (compare 1 Cor. 9:24–27). Some of these Jewish Christian believers may have been looking rather wistfully at their Jewish neighbours and friends whose homes had not been plundered and who did not seem to be paying a price for their faith. A carefully selected Scripture reminds them that sonship implies discipline. They must not lose courage (5) when hardship comes. The corrective experiences of life are proof of God's love (6), not evidence of his neglect. The early Christian preacher, John Chrysostom, says that 'it is those things in which they suppose they have been deserted by God that should make them confident that they have not been deserted'. Abraham (6:15), Moses (11:27) and Jesus (12:2,3) 'endured' and so must they (7b). The disciple recognises the necessity of discipline; it is an essential part of the learning process. God's correction far transcends that which is exercised by human parents. They discipline 'at their pleasure' (10); although well-meaning, it may not always take the best form or focus on the appropriate remedy. But 'the Father of spirits' always works 'for our good'. Although initially painful, it will prove ultimately beneficial (Ps. 119:67,71).

THOUGHT: If we want to 'share his holiness' (10), then we must be subject to his training. The ploughshare may occasionally cut deep, but there will be an abundant harvest, 'the peaceful fruit of righteousness' (11). Those who agonise as Christian gymnasts (11, *gegumnasmenois*, 'trained') will enjoy the 'peaceful' blessings of eventual victory. The fruit of righteousness is the victor's crown (2 Tim. 4:8).

12:12–17 Away with despondency

In view of the fact that present or impending adversity may well prove to be the best possible expression of God's loving (and not hostile) purposes, these believers must not be overwhelmed, fearful or discouraged at the prospect of suffering. This is not a time for downheartedness; they must lift their 'drooping hands'. A power beyond their own will enable them to stiffen those 'weak knees'. This imagery is surely meant to recall Isaiah 35:3,4 with its encouragement to those of a 'fearful heart'. The Christian life demands something more than passive acceptance of disciplinary correction. They must not only put up with adversity; they must press on and 'make straight paths' for themselves (a quotation from the Septuagint version of Prov. 4:26). This is not simply for their own spiritual progress, but so that the 'lame' members of this church may not be made worse by their poor example but 'healed' as they look on those who run well in the race.

Nothing does more to disrupt congregational harmony than a breach in relationships. Believers have to 'strive' for peace; it does not come automatically. The sons of God are peace-makers (Matt. 5:9), not merely peace-keepers, and certainly not peace-breakers. It is a creative activity, motivated, inspired and preserved by the God of peace (13:20; Rom 15:33), the Lord Jesus who is our peace (Eph. 2:14,15,17), and the Spirit who produces it (Gal. 5:22) as miraculous fruit in our otherwise turbulent lives. And note that it is 'peace with all men', not simply with those you get along happily with anyway! Calvin is surely right when he says that 'this cannot happen unless we forget many injuries and show each other natural forgiveness in many things'.

Believers must also strive for holiness of life, procured for us in Christ (1 Cor. 1:30); the longing to see him one day face to face (14) will provide inspiration and correction as well as motivation (1 John 3:2,3). In his teaching about the church our writer has an acute sense of corporate responsibility. A believer's failure to pursue the way of holiness (Isa. 35 again) can have a defiling effect on others as well as himself. The worldly-minded or careless Christian, or worse, the determined apostate, can seriously disturb the spiritual life of the local Christian community. The quotation used at this point recalls the infectious effect of an idolator's presence in Mosaic times (Deut. 29:18,19).

REMEMBER: Although he belonged to a believing family, Esau allowed the pleasure of the moment (16; Gen 25:24–34) to rob him of the blessings of the future (17; Gen. 27:30–40). His bad example is here presented as a warning about apostasy. Lured by immediate prosperity, those who reject eternal values invite future loss.

12:18–24 Two mountains

Lest these readers become overwhelmed by the serious warnings which have just been issued (15–17), they are reminded (with the aid of another brilliant contrast-picture) that in Christ they are no longer under law but under grace (compare 2:2–4). They do not stand trembling at the foot of Sinai, conscious of its deep darkness and rigid unapproachable boundaries. They have come to a better mountain. Sinai spelt death to those who ignored its warnings; those who come to Mount Zion, the city of the living God, receive life (compare 12:9; John 10:10). Under the old covenant, believers were told to keep away (Exod. 19:12–24); under the new they are urged to draw near (4:16; 10:22). At Sinai even the best of men (21) was terrified; through Christ even the worst of men can have peace (Luke 23:39–43; Rom. 5:6–11; 1 Tim. 1:13,14). When the law thundered out men begged that nothing further might be said (19; Exod. 20:18,19); transformed by grace, believers crave for more (John 6:34).

For all its rich historical associations, the earthly Jerusalem was not easily accessible for most Jewish believers, but the 'heavenly Jerusalem' is the place where all Christians have now arrived, surrounded by the adoring angels, accompanied by the earlier saints (now 'made perfect') and, best of all, welcomed by a better mediator than Moses (Deut. 5:5). His sprinkled blood does not cry for vengeance (24; Gen. 4:10); it speaks of mercy. The 'Judge' of men is the God of 'all', arrogant, Christ-rejecting Gentiles as well as fearfully submissive Jews at Sinai, Old Testament believers as well as New Testament saints. All are accountable to him and all are moving to that Day when the books will be opened. Those whose names are 'enrolled in heaven' (23) are better than those whose achievements are extolled on earth.

The graphic portraiture of these verses, with their present encouragement as well as future expectation, has an intensely practical purpose. With that same pastoral skill we have noted earlier, he is begging them to press on to the glories that are yet to be. How foolish to 'shrink back' when they have come so far. What folly to return to Sinai when Zion is on the horizon. The 'first-born' (23) are those entitled to the father's special blessing; how foolish to be like Esau (16,17) and lose it.

THOUGHT: In his exposition of this passage Charles A. Trentham reminds us that the blood of the Lord Jesus 'speaks more graciously than the blood of Abel' because 'it is the blood of him who ever intercedes for us and pleads his sacrifice as the ground of our forgiveness'.

12:25-29 Worship with reverence

The multitude of terror-stricken Hebrews, who looked up to Sinai in that fierce storm, stopped their ears to the overwhelming word of a holy God (19; Exod. 20:19). They said that if they heard his voice any more they would die (Deut. 5:25,26). Deliberately recalling these stark exodus events, our writer wants to make the point that only by hearing and obeying that voice can we live (25). In a similar context, the giving of the law, he returns here to the warning of judgement he gave at the beginning of the letter (2:1-3). With an understandable desire to present the Christian gospel winsomely and attractively, the Christian is always in danger of neglecting, obscuring or minimising the biblical doctrine of judgement. Man's accountability to God is a theme found throughout both Old and New Testaments; to ignore these warnings in our presentation of Christian truth is seriously to distort the gospel. After all, the fact that God warns man is a clear indication of his loving desire for our salvation (2 Pet. 3:9). But those who will not have Christ as Saviour must meet him as Judge. There is a warning, to preachers especially, in the words of Thomas Hooker, one of the New England Puritans, 'You who think that Christ is made all of mercy, it is a God of your own imagination, and your own devising.'

From the narrative in Exodus our writer moves naturally and perceptively to a prophecy by Haggai (26; Hag. 2:6). The shaking of Sinai anticipates a day when everything will be shaken, not only the earth beneath our feet, but the entire universe. As the letter draws to its close its author has seized again on a theme found in its introduction (1:11,12). The Day when all existence will be shaken will reveal the great unshakable realities, a sovereign God, the unchanging Christ and his secure people. An awareness of the coming Day ought to issue in practical consequences. It will inspire our gratitude (28a). How privileged we are to belong to a God who will keep us as his treasured possession for ever. It will motivate our worship (28b). We will not wish simply to be among the entire creation who, whether they like it or not, will bow before him in subjugation (Phil. 2:10,11). Believers voluntarily anticipate that great event by bringing their willing worship whenever they can.

REMEMBER: Without proper care, our rightful intimacy with God is always in danger of degenerating into a flippant attitude, inappropriate language, careless conversation, spiritual indifference. Although Sinai is no longer aflame (18), the consuming fire of God's holy and righteous love burns on (Deut. 4:24; Isa. 33:14).

13:1–6 Love never fails

The 'holy' (3:1) brothers and sisters who make up this congregation and whose family relationship brings constant delight to the heart of God (2:11; compare 11:16) are urged to ensure that their 'love' is a *continuing* (1) demonstration of their unity in Christ and not an occasional or spasmodic urge to express their affection. It must issue in practical deeds and not be left on the uncostly level of mere sentimentality. True love opens the doors of our homes to others (as Abraham welcomed messengers of mercy centuries earlier, Gen. 18: 1–15) and it knocks on prison doors as a compassionate visitor (3).

The exhortation not to forget the prisoners ought not to be passed over quickly as though it belonged only to the world of antiquity. Remember, as you read this, that there are many believers, especially in the USSR, who can no longer live with their families simply because of their loyalty to Christ and rightful desire for freedom to share their faith with others. Grateful for our religious liberty, we ought to pray and work for those who do not enjoy this freedom.

Some of this church's members appear to have been physically assaulted; 'those who are being maltreated' (3, NEB) still claim a place in our prayers. These early Christian churches were particularly sensitive to the needs of fellow Christians in their own, neighbouring and even distant (1 Pet. 5:9) churches. Have we become comfortably insular, or even totally careless, about our suffering brethren in other parts of the world?

Marital love comes next (4); the Judge who is God of all (12:23) will not overlook immoral conduct and infidelity. In a day like our own, when marriage breakdown has become an accepted feature of contemporary social life, every Christian home can be a model of love and loyalty, security and stability.

The 'love of money' has ruined many a marriage. Love for God and for each other is a far more rewarding quest. Contentment is one of life's greatest treasures. Once again, the Old Testament is used to support the argument and strengthen the appeal. When Joshua was promised the divine presence, he inherited a blessing greater than anything money could buy (5; Josh. 1:5), whilst later the psalmist realised that with the Lord as his helper (as well as his companion), all his fears were banished.

THOUGHT: Notice the delightful comment here about God's word and our recurrent testimony to its truth: 'he has said . . . Hence we can confidently say' (5b,6). Richard Sibbes, the seventeenth-century Puritan, was surely right when he affirmed that 'there is no other principle to prove the word, but experience from the working of it'.

13:7–14 Bearing the stigma that he bore

At a time when, because of cruelty (3), immorality (4), avarice (5) and heresy (9), it was difficult for some of these believers to hold fast to their confession (10:23), they are urged to look back to the example of their former leaders (7), whose heroism and sanctity are an enduring inspiration, and look up to the Lord Jesus, their unchanging friend (8). Christ is their unfailing contemporary. The letter began with a clear reference to his changeless nature (1:12) and it closes on the same note of encouraging affirmation.

From time to time the people of God are harassed by false teachers, as well as edified by good ones. Not every leader shares the word of God (7) by which all truth must be tested. These purveyors of 'diverse and strange teachings' (9) may have been Jewish (see 9:10) or gnostic (Col. 2:16) propagandists who insisted on the meticulous observance of food laws of one kind or another. This pastor appeals again to the superiority of 'inwardness' over ceremonial observance or legalistic regulations. The reference to 'those who serve the tent' (i.e. tabernacle) suggests that it is some Jewish ritual or dietary restriction which has been introduced.

To be 'strengthened by grace' is to be fortified against ills of every kind, false teaching or anything else. We have a better altar than any which was served by the Levitical priesthood. It is clear from the context that the word 'altar' here (10) 'is a sort of shorthand . . . for the whole sacrificial action of Christ' (Philip Hughes). On the Day of Atonement the bodies of the sacrificial victims were burned outside the camp, and on that first Good Friday 'Jesus also suffered outside the gate'. He was cast out of the city, despised and unwanted, by those who rejected his kingship and who longed for his death (John 19:15). In the same way these believers must be prepared to go out 'to him' (note not 'for him'), outside the safe confines of Judaism. William Manson has made the suggestion that Hebrews was written not to a church threatened by apostasy, but a congregation in danger of cowardice. Afraid of possible persecution, these Jewish Christians may have kept quiet about their distinctively Christian faith and have found it more safe to live 'in the Jewish part of their Christianity'.

THOUGHT: Like the conclusion to Matthew's Gospel, these closing verses remind their readers that to meet Christ and hear his 'Lo, I am with you' (Matt. 28: 18–20), we must go out into the Christ-rejecting world. A sense of the Lord's presence may well be reserved for witnesses (13) and pilgrims (14).

13:15–25 Assurance for the flock

Rejoicing in Christ's sacrifice, Christians do not speak boastfully about sacrifices they have made. But Scripture says that there are sacrifices for them to offer (15,16; compare Rom. 12:1). The 'sacrifice of praise' is not merely vocal. The lips that 'acknowledge his name' in unashamed confession are eager also to obey his orders about sharing their possessions. These sacrifices are more pleasing to him than ceremonial observances. The desire to obey God's Word will mean that we are attentive to those who teach it (17), though this exhortation is certainly not intended to encourage an undiscerning kind of submission. After all, not every teacher had the truth (9), so everything must always be subjected to the truth of Scripture, the teaching itself and the lives of those who teach. God's servant is accountable to him and for this reason he will always be 'keeping watch' like a vigilant sentry or a faithful shepherd. Our writer certainly does not want to lord it over this congregation. He casts himself on their prayers (18,19) and concludes by praying for them in the most comprehensive of all benedictions (20,21). He longs that 'the God of peace' might bring harmony to what may have been a divided congregation (12:13–15). The power that raised Christ from the dead is surely adequate for their needs. They are Christ's flock, bound to him in covenant bonds which cannot be broken. The promise to equip them with 'everything good' is heartening and uplifting, especially for any readers of the letter who may have been convicted by its teaching. The word translated 'equip' (*katartizō*) literally means 'to put into a proper condition'. It is also used to describe the work of restoration and necessary repair. When Jesus first met those fishermen by Galilee they were 'mending' (*katartizontas*) their nets. God is able to repair what is broken in our lives and supply those things which, at the moment, are lacking. But note that there is a condition here. Those who wish to be supplied with necessary grace and restored to what they ought to be must obey ('do his will'), please and glorify him. This 'brief' letter of exhortation (22) concludes with a reminder that in every century Christian workers have been supported not only by gifted colleagues (23,24), but by unlimited grace (25).

THOUGHT: If this letter's 'word of exhortation' (22) has corrected or rebuked you, do not be resentful. 'Sharp though it be, and to the flesh tiresome, yet suffer it. Better it is that the vine should bleed than die.' (John Trapp)

Questions for further study and discussion on Hebrews 12 and 13

1. When Christ 'endured the cross', what exactly was 'the joy that was set before him' (12:2)? Meditate on the comment that *'because of the joy'* (GNB) can also be translated *'instead of'*. The 'joy' here might refer to the perfect communion of the pre-existent Christ with his Father. Why did he exchange all that for the hostility of sinners (12:3)?

2. Does the teaching of 12:4–11 encourage us to distinguish between God's corrective discipline and life's inevitable adversities?

3. How can we guard against irreverence (12:28)?

4. In the light of the teaching on 13:2–5, consider the various ministries open to anyone with a Christian home.

5. How does one reconcile the exhortation of 13:17 about submitting to leaders (compare 1 Cor. 16:16; 1 Thess. 5:12,13; 1 Pet. 5:5) with references like Galatians 5:13, Ephesians 5:21; Philippians 2:3,4, which insist on the importance of mutual submission? Is it possible that the first set of references guard against disrespect and the second against tyranny?

6. What are the effects of a 'root of bitterness' (12:15)? How can we guard against it?

7. Use your imagination to 'get inside' the contrasts of 12:18–24. Which does your worship most closely resemble? What would you change?

8. What might going to him 'outside the camp' (13:13) mean in practice? Are you doing it? How *can* we do it?

James : Introduction

Martin Luther described this letter as 'a right strawy epistle', comparing it unfavourably with those New Testament letters which had made a greater appeal to his mind in a time of spiritual crisis, epistles like Romans, Galatians and Ephesians: 'These are the books which show you Christ and teach you everything that is needful.' In the course of our lives, certain books of the Bible may well come to mean more to us than others, but *all* Scripture is necessary for our instruction, rebuke and encouragement, and to neglect any part is to expose ourselves to doctrinal imbalance, moral indifference or spiritual neglect. It is easy to understand why Luther wrote as he did. In 1519 his Catholic opponent, John Eck, had used James 2:17 against the reformer and from that time on Luther was always hesitant about the value of the epistle. But we are on firmer ground in this matter if, with Paul, we acknowledge the importance of 'the whole counsel of God' (Acts 20:27). Throughout Christian history the epistle of James has reminded its readers of the necessity of good Christian conduct as an expression of sound Christian doctrine. Committed Christians know that they are likely to influence people as much by what they do as by what they say.

The contents of this letter assume even greater value when one realises that so many of Christ's sayings are echoed in it, e.g. Matt. 5:7; 18:33–35 (2:13); Matt. 5:48 (1:4); Matt. 7:7,8 (1:5; 4:2); Matt. 7:11 (1:5,17); Matt. 7:21–27 (1:22–25; 4:17); Matt. 21:22 (1:6); Mark 12:31 (2:8); Luke 6:20–23 (2:5); and there are similar echoes in James 3:12; 4:4,6,10,11–12,13–17; 5:2–3,7–9,12. This dependence on and reminder of the sayings of Jesus is natural if the author of the letter is, as many believe, our Lord's brother of that name (Matt. 13:55; Acts 12:17; 15:13; 1 Cor. 15:7; Gal. 1:19; 2:9).

We cannot dogmatise about the date of the letter and various suggestions from AD 50 onwards have been made. Possibly a date in the mid–60s of the first century might best suit its message. By then James may have become aware of these Judaisers who were raising forceful objections to Paul's doctrine of justification by grace through faith (Rom. 3,4; Gal. 3). James may well be using this letter to make some necessary comments not only on the 'faith and works' theme, but also about the necessity of consistent daily behaviour. Expounding the letter in a time of adversity, the seventeenth-century preacher, Thomas Manton, said that *James* is 'fraught with excellent instructions, how to bear afflictions, to hear the word, to mortify the vile affections, to bridle the tongue, to conceive rightly of the nature of God, to adorn our profession with a good conversation, with meekness and peace and charity.'

Analysis of James

1:1–8 Joy in trials

At the beginning of this intensely practical letter, James deals with two qualities of great importance both to first-century and modern readers, steadfastness (2–4) and wisdom (5–8); what to do and where to look when you are tested. His opening salutation (1) reminds his readers that he is God's submissive slave and that, as 'the twelve tribes' (a natural adoption of Old Testament imagery to describe the New Testament scattered church, compare 1 Pet. 2:9,10), they are God's secure possession; obedience and confidence are essential aspects of healthy discipleship.

The first readers of the epistle were under some pressure. Nobody enjoys 'trials', but James insists that good things emerge from them. Bacon said that as prosperity is the blessing of the Old Testament, adversity is that of the New. It never arrives as a solitary visitor. The Christian knows that rich qualities always accompany it, as well as resources which can scarcely be discovered in any other way. It must be received with joy (2); some gold may be found in the darkest places of life. For one thing, it will demonstrate the reality of our faith. Anyone can believe when everything is happy; continuance in faith even in bewildering hardship shows that it is genuine and not 'fair weather' faith. The trials (*peirasmos*) are but tests as a young bird tests (*peirazein*) its wings; you will hardly know how buoyant you are until trouble comes. The 'testing' (a word used elsewhere to describe sterling coinage) will take the form of 'various' (literally, 'many coloured') trials but, rightly handled, they will produce fortitude. 'Steadfastness' (same word as at 5:11 and found in Luke 21:19; Rom. 5:3; 1 Cor. 13:7; Heb. 10:36) can only come through trouble. Moreover, constancy in trials increases spiritual maturity. It will lead to completeness, an adequate faith without glaring deficiencies.

The tested man will need great wisdom (see 3:17) to handle life's difficult experiences creatively. 'And if . . . any of you does not know how to meet any particular problem' (5, J. B. Phillips) wisdom is given, but only to the man who prays (5), by a generous God who gives his blessings ungrudgingly and not as we deserve them. The faith which is uncomplaining in trials is the faith that cries for help (6), an unwavering faith which knows persistence in prayer as well as perseverance in trouble. The opposite to this kind of steady reliance is uncertain doubt, like a cork floating on the wave (Mayor). It is not only wisdom which will be withheld from such a 'double-minded' (compare 4:8) man; people with divided loyalties end up with nothing in their hands (8).

A THOUGHT FOR TODAY: 'Grace grows best in winter' (Samuel Rutherford).

1:9–18 The word of life

Just as the tested man should count his blessings, so should the poor member; his spiritual wealth is incalculable (9; 2:5; compare Matt. 6:19–21; 2 Cor. 6:10; 8:9), whereas the rich man's possessions (all perishable as scorched grass, 10,11; Isa. 40:6–8; 1 Pet. 1:24) will, like their owner, 'fade away' and at the moment when he is engaged in further 'pursuits' (11) – travels, possibly business journeys to increase his capital. Whether our trials are financial or otherwise, the man with endurance, wisdom from God and love for God, will ultimately receive the greatest of all treasures (12).

The link between ideas which James places together is sometimes found in a key word; here it is the idea of 'testing' which emerges again. James wants to make it clear that it has two forms; there is the test of faith (3) which God uses and the test of temptation to evil which God does not initiate (13). The two must be clearly distinguished. Although James obviously does not doubt that the devil tempts (see Mark 1:13; Luke 22:31; 1 Pet. 5:8), he here focuses on the allurement of man's own selfish desires – possibly, in this context (11), the enticement of increased possessions which prove attractive because of man's covetous nature. It all follows a sick regression; man is enticed (the original words describe the use of bait in hunting or fishing, 14b) by his own selfish desire, producing, if unchecked, the sin which ends in death. God does not initiate this grim process. He is the giver of everything good, not evil. The Creator of 'lights' is unvariable – not as the sun, 'now the full light of noon, now the dimness of twilight, and at night no light at all' (Ropes), but as the unchanging Father. The words in verse 17b can be variously translated, but the general idea is that our God is utterly unchangeable in his nature and is likewise incapable of being deflected from his purposes by anyone else. God's 'word of truth' (18) brings us into new life so that believers become those who are completely dedicated to God's purposes, as the 'first fruits' (i.e. the best, Num. 18:12) in Old Testament times were devoted entirely to him and were therefore 'holy' (Exod. 23:19; Lev. 23:10).

THOUGHT: Thank God today for his most perfect gift to us, his utterly truthful word (18; Eph. 1:13; Col. 1:5). It is as unchanging as the one who has given it in his sovereignty ('of his own will'). Accept what he has said and show your gratitude by obeying it.

1:19–27 A word to obey

Some of life's greatest 'trials' come not through what we lack (money, compare 9–11) but through what others say (19,20). James is later to devote considerable space to this theme (3:1–12; 4:11). Hearing God's perfect (25) word is infinitely preferable to speaking our words which may either express or arouse anger, and this will hardly further God's righteous purposes. We all tend to talk far too much (Prov. 10:19). One Jewish Rabbi said, 'Silence is a fence for Wisdom', and the Old Testament wisdom literature has a good deal to say on the subject (e.g. Prov. 12:13; 13:3; 18:21; Eccl. 3:7; 5:2,3). Putting away evil (21), literally as dirty clothes (see Eph. 4:22,25, repentance), and receiving and believing the engrafted word (faith) issues in salvation (21b). But the word must not merely be heard but obeyed (22–25). The vivid 'mirror' illustration portrays the casual or forgetful reader who does not relate what he sees in the word to what he sees his own need to be. James here presents us with another of his many memorable contrast pictures. We have already had the steadfast and unstable man, the rich and the poor, the test which God uses (2,3) and the test which man fails (14,15); here we have the hearer who forgets and the doer who acts (25). In the remaining verses of the chapter (26,27) he comments on three of his major practical themes – controlled speech (26), compassionate service (27a) and personal holiness (27b). A man's 'religion' (the word refers primarily to the outward aspects of faith, public worship, etc.) is vain if it is not given expression in the everyday world. A person who only 'thinks he is religious' but is not genuinely Christian in every part of his life, will neither satisfy himself ('deceives his heart'), help others (visit the needy who are of special concern to the Lord he professes to serve, Deut. 14:29; Isa. 1:17), or please God. Impractical religion is 'defiled' by this sort of inadequacy, but those who have practised it can be cleansed (Isa. 1:16–18) and the cleansing is not an isolated spiritual event locked away in the past. Even in the squalid environment of the first (and twentieth) century believers are kept 'unstained' by the God who not only demands purity, but makes it possible (1 Pet. 1:14–16; 1 John 1:7–9).

THOUGHT: Is there some lonely or needy person in your neighbourhood who you ought to visit as an unobtrusive but important expression of your 'pure and undefiled' faith?

2:1–7 Rich in faith

With his rightful insistence on practical Christianity, James turns from his brief general reference to the rich and poor to a particular example of glaring inequality in a place where it ought never to be seen, the local church. Those who have a 'pure' religion (i.e. acceptable in God's sight (1:27) will not 'judge' (4b) people by their dress or jewellery (2) but by their spiritual wealth (5). Those who show 'partiality' (1) in this way have forgotten that during his earthly ministry 'the Lord of glory' they profess to follow had special care for the poor and helpless. Look at the central section of *Luke* and notice how compassionately the Lord Jesus gave himself to people who were either a nuisance or troublesome, unwanted, neglected or feared, people like hungry travellers, humanly incurable epileptics, helpless mutes, despised Samaritans, ostracised lepers, blind beggars, dishonest tax-collectors (all these appear in chs. 9–19).

James says that if church members have put their faith *in* Christ (1, that is the meaning here), it is unfitting to dishonour (6) those whom Christ loves and God has chosen (5). We are not their judges; they are our brethren (notice how the word is repeated in the passage, 1,5). If they love *him* (5b), surely we ought also to love *them* (8). The reference to oppressive measures adopted by the rich (6) suggests that James has in mind here the affluent unbelievers of first-century society, not believers. Such people are not only greedy and loveless, but also blasphemers. This passage needs to be studied carefully by contemporary Christians. In many churches and Christian organisations a man with a good job is much more likely to be appointed to office than a man with a rich faith. A man or woman can have both of course, but one fears that, almost unconsciously, external factors sometimes determine the choice: 'He's not very well-known.' 'A person with a larger home could do more entertaining.' 'We've never had a black deacon before.' 'I don't really think it's a woman's job.' Today's passage is strikingly relevant in our pathetically divided society.

THOUGHT: God is not impressed by gold rings and fine clothing (2). He looks deeper. Remember how he passed by Jesse's strong and tall sons in order to find the one with the right heart (see 1 Sam. 16:6–13).

2:8–13 Be merciful to me . . .

In these verses James weaves together two of his favourite themes, obedience to the word (1:22) and love for others (5,6; compare 1:27b). He insists that we should love our poor neighbour, not only because 'the Lord of glory' did so (1), but because God's word commands it (8). Study the context of that quotation in Leviticus (19:9–18) and notice how particularly appropriate it is with its references to a number of issues already raised by James, care for the needy, improper speech, blaspheming or profaning the Lord's name, undue deference to the great to the neglect of the poor. Our author is opposed to selective obedience. There are those who glory in the fact that they have kept one commandment, but what is the point of that if they have broken others (10,11)?

To show 'partiality' or be guilty of favouritism is to break the 'royal law', 'the Law of the Great King' (John Wesley) and, perhaps more in mind here, the law which governs those who have entered his kingdom. If we practise this form of unloving discrimination we are disregarding God's kingship (8), disobeying his word, offending his holiness (9, 'you commit sin') and forgetting his judgement (12). James has already referred to the 'law of liberty' (1:25) and he repeats the description here (12). Here is a law which 'liberates us from the lustful pull of our own nature' (Motyer) and 'enables men to find their true freedom in the service of God's will' (Tasker). The law which has been our guide in matters of speech and conduct (12) will become our judge. The closing verse in today's passage is one of the many occasions in this letter when we meet a saying clearly reminiscent of the teaching of Christ, possibly the brother of our writer. Verse 13 echoes the sayings of Jesus in Matthew 18:32–35; Luke 6:37,38; compare Matthew 5:7. There are many other examples and similar instances in the letter, and searching them out (and obeying their injunctions!) is a rewarding experience. What a glorious thing it is that, even with its shattering exposure of human sinfulness, particularly in relationships, and its stark warnings, this passage ends on the note of promised mercy; if God manifests mercy to us we ought surely to show it towards others.

THOUGHT: 'To break one commandment is to break all, for it is to violate the principle of obedience, just as it matters not at what particular point a man breaks his way out of an enclosure, if he is forbidden to go out of it at all' (F. W. Farrar).

2:14–26 Faith and works

In his discussion of practical love for the needy, James moves naturally from discrimination against the poor (1–5) and lovelessness toward them (8) to their practical necessities, not only a loving welcome at church (whatever they happen to be wearing), but also the provision of their daily food and adequate clothing. Some people can be indifferent to this kind of need or piously dismiss it with an appropriate verse or prayer (16). The example James provides of this kind of 'faith without works' takes us to the heart of one of his major themes and one which some have found puzzling in the light of Paul's dismissal of 'works' as a means of salvation (Eph. 2:9). It is important to see that both Paul and James use the terms 'faith' and 'works' in a rather different sense.

When Paul talks about 'faith' he usually means utter commitment to Christ. James sometimes means that (e.g. v. 1), but not always. He occasionally means 'belief' in the sense of believing or accepting the fact of God's existence, in that sense even the devils 'believe' in him (19). James' idea of 'works' is different too. The 'works' scornfully dismissed by Paul are ceremonial or moral deeds performed in the hope of purchasing salvation. The unique 'work' of Christ brought all that to an end as a means of achieving righteousness (Rom. 10:3,4; Phil. 3:9). But Paul did not minimise the importance of works as a way of expressing the new life we already have in Christ. Far from it. We are not accepted by God *because* of works', but we are 'created in Christ Jesus *for* good works' (Eph. 2:9,10), and these are the 'works' which James describes here. In a sense, what James means by 'works', Paul describes as 'fruit' (Gal. 5:22,23). Abraham did not merely believe in God's existence, nor simply trust what God had said. He acted upon it and did what God told him to do, costly as it was (21). He was a doer of the word if ever there was one. And from righteous Abraham our author moves to unrighteous Rahab (25), from the man to the woman, the Jew to the Gentile, the rich to the poor, the spiritually privileged to the morally corrupt. She did not have Abraham's religious background but, hearing about God's power (Josh. 2:9–11), she acted upon God's word (Josh. 2:18,21; 6:17; Heb. 11:31).

REMEMBER: The friends of God (23b) obey the word of God; they have a *living* faith (26).

Questions for further study and discussion on James 1 and 2

1. Describe some of the other blessings which come out of 'trials' apart from the 'steadfastness' mentioned by James in 1:3,4. How will these other qualities also serve to make us 'complete, lacking in nothing'?

2. We know that 'God . . . himself tempts no one' (1:13), but why did he, though omnipotent, allow sinful desires to gain such a firm foothold in humanity when he knew, as omniscient Lord, they would have such devastating results?

3. Both Paul (1 Tim. 4:4; 6:17) and James (1:17) refer to the good things which God has given to us like, presumably, food, drink, human love, scientific skills (to name but a few) which can be pathetically or even tragically misused as well as enjoyed. Is it ever right deliberately to deny oneself something which God has given and meant to be 'received with thanksgiving'? If not, how do we relate these verses to issues like Western gluttony and world hunger, the serious rise in the number of alcoholics, sexual permissiveness and 'the arms race'?

4. Could you and your fellow church members summon enough courage to make an honest examination of your own church life in the light of 2:1–13?

5. How does one relate the message of 2:14–26 to the fact that every day vast numbers of our contemporaries die of starvation? What practical steps can you take towards 'giving them the things needed for the body'?

6. What does James 1:5–7 have to say about the 'problem of unanswered prayer'? Are there other biblical principles that you feel would have to be included in order to give a complete answer?

7. We normally speak as though Satan was responsible for all temptation. Would James agree? Are there any dangers in our approach?

8. Covetousness and partiality are perhaps two of the most common and socially acceptable sins of our day. How do they show themselves – in your community, in your church, in yourself?

3:1–5 Small and dangerous

Some of the scattered churches (1:1) James is addressing seem also to have been unhappy churches, troubled by biting speech (1:19,20), unbecoming behaviour (1:21), social discrimination (2:1–13) and the heartless dismissal of needy people (2:15,16). It is possible to glamorise the church of the New Testament period forgetting that, like ourselves, its members were saved sinners (1 Tim. 1:15) as well as 'saints'. Now we meet a new problem in the letter, that of the lust for power or authority (1) without the recognition that the teaching office also makes great demands. A number of people must have been pressing for a place of leadership within these local congregations.

The spiritual leader needs a sanctified tongue. More will be expected of him both by his contemporaries and by his Lord (1b). No man is infallible, but the man who never says anything wrong must get very near to it (2). With graphic and unforgettable illustration, James makes constructive use of his own tongue when, dictating this letter (as most New Testament writers did, 1 Pet. 5:12), he describes what can happen when our speech is not surrendered to Christ. The power of the tongue is utterly out of proportion to its size. Like the small bit in the strong horse's mouth, the tiny rudder of a great ship, the insignificant little fire which eventually consumes an entire forest, the tongue has enormous potential for good or evil. The reference to the tongue's tendency to *boast* (5,14) anticipates the strong things this letter has to say later about *pride* (4:6–10) which expresses itself in selfish ambition (14), bitter relationships (4:1,2), unashamed worldliness (4:4), self-opinionated arrogance (4:11,12) and human presumption (4:13–17). Most of this havoc is caused or fostered by sins of speech.

Unkind gossip has probably done more damage in Christian communities than almost any other human failure. To say damaging things about another person is to release a dangerous missile which can only hurt and cause destructive havoc.

'Who steals my purse steals trash;'tis something, nothing:
'Twas mine,'tis his, and has been slave to thousands;
But he that filches from me my good name
Robs me of that which not enriches him,
And makes me poor indeed.' (Shakespeare, *Othello*)

GIVE THANKS TO GOD for those men and women whose sanctified conversation has been of particular blessing to you. What made their speech so effective in your Christian life?

3:6–12 The tongue is a fire

James continues to drive his point home. More than good illustration (3–5) is necessary for effective communication; the teacher must practise repetition as well (Phil. 3:1b). He has already suggested that it is impossible to estimate the tongue's influence; now he goes on to say that it is difficult to control its power. 'Fire' describes its destructive effect (6). The carelessly spoken word can seriously pollute ('staining', same idea as 1:27b) the life of the one who says it, let alone those it reaches. The unsanctified tongue has devilish potential (where 'hell' is a personification used of the devil as 'heaven' is sometimes used for 'God'). It is like a wild beast not easily tamed (7), a restless evil; 'it will not stay still. Even its echoes can kill, when the original speaker is silent' (Ronald Ward, *New Bible Commentary Revised*, IVP). It can bite like a vicious snake 'full of deadly poison' (8b; compare Ps. 140:3; Rom. 3:13) and be guilty of glaring (yet unacknowledged) hypocrisy (9–12).

Behind this devastating imagery, James is imaginatively presenting the positive side as well. By his use of the underground spring and fruit-tree illustrations (11,12), he is eager to recognise the potential of the tongue as well as its destructive power, its ability to do good as well as evil. The determined rider will see that the bit guides his horse in the right direction. The skilful pilot uses the rudder well. Even the spark can be used for good purposes. The prayer or hymn with which we bless God is acceptable if genuine. Pure water can be refreshing and good fruit a delight. There is surely another echo here (12) of the teaching of Jesus in Matt. 7:15–20 which is, after all, about people like false prophets who do not use their tongues aright and those who take the Lord's name upon their lips but are not doers of the word (Matt. 7:21–27). It is certainly true that 'no human being can tame the tongue' (8), but the Lord can. Contrast Peter's speech before and after his surrender to Christ. Guile was certainly 'found on his lips' and, unlike his Master, when he was reviled he reviled in return (Matt. 26:69–75; 1 Pet. 2:22,23; compare 3:9–11,15). Later that same tongue preached eloquently and persuasively to thousands (Acts 2:37–41). In the power of Christ the tongue can not only be tamed but used.

A PRAYER: Take my voice, and let me sing
Always, only, for my King:
Take my lips, and let them be
Filled with messages from Thee.
(Frances Ridley Havergal)

3:13–18 Two kinds of wisdom

Believing in necessary repetition, our gifted teacher returns (13) to his earlier themes of wisdom and works. Further contrast pictures are drawn in this section between earthly (15) and heavenly (17) wisdom, between selfish rivalry (14) and merciful (17), peace-making (18) works. It is an example of brilliant compression; teachers who have to be repetitive do not have to be long-winded. It reads more like a series of excellent sermon notes meant to be expounded in every church where the letter was read.

The 'good life' (as opposed to the fiercely destructive one described in the previous verses) is one where wisdom is not marred by intellectual pride, but is characterised by 'meekness' as demonstrated in the life of the best and most effective teacher the world has ever known (Matt. 11:29). God deliberately withholds his wisdom from those who cannot use it with humility (Matt. 11:25; 1 Cor. 1:19–31). Those who lack wisdom and do not live the 'good life' are jealous of the success of others and are ambitious for themselves (14,16). They are boastful about what knowledge (or anything else) they possess and their daily behaviour is a direct denial of the truth they profess; this is probably the meaning of 'false to the truth' (14b).

One can easily see that these serious failings would be specially harmful if manifest in teachers. The extended section on the tongue does, after all, arise from a reference to ambitious leaders (1). James may well be returning to the 'leadership' theme in these verses. Certainly there were harmful rivalries in these churches (4:1,11) and, if the troubles are to be healed, earthly wisdom will not simply be useless; being 'devilish' (15) it will actually make things worse (16). The wisdom which God gives to the praying, believing (1:5,6) leader will be of an entirely different order, *pure*, not wicked (1:21); *peaceable*, not angry (1:19); *gentle*, not assertive (3:1); *open to reason*, not boastful (14) about its own opinions; *full of mercy*, not indifferent (2:16); a life with *good fruits* (2:26), convinced and sincere. Such a 'good life' produces an abundant harvest, righteousness before God and peace with men (18). The making of peace is a spiritual art, inspired and sustained by our peace-loving Triune God (Heb. 13:20; Eph. 2:14; Gal. 5:22). In times like our own, when there is so much rivalry, disharmony and bitterness, the Christian has a unique opportunity to exercise his responsibility as a peace-maker (Matt. 5:9).

PRAYER: Lord, make us instruments of thy peace. Where there is hatred, let us sow love; where there is injury, pardon; where there is discord, union; where there is doubt, faith; where there is despair, hope; where there is darkness, light; where there is sadness, joy; for thy mercy and for thy truth's sake.

4:1–4 Unfaithful creatures

One of the many remarkable things about the Bible is its stark honesty. As we have seen already, the portraiture of the church in the New Testament is not an account of utterly blameless conduct. James has already referred to some very disappointing features in the lives of the churches he is addressing and now we discover that some members are not only quarrelsome but also covetous, aggressive in their relationships, worldly and guilty of a seriously defective prayer life.

It is hardly likely that the 'killing' referred to here is meant to be taken literally. First-century congregations (like contemporary ones) could be guilty of some great failings, but murder did not rank high among them. This is another of James's unforgettable contrast pictures. On the one hand there is the thoroughly worldly existence, a life controlled and dominated by the human passions fiercely striving within the individual man or woman (1:14,15) and expressing themselves in harmful behaviour towards others. On the other there is the pure, peaceable, gentle, merciful life just described in the previous verses. Some Christians may even have been adversely influenced by the violent attitudes of some zealots in first-century Palestinian Judaism (e.g. Mark 15:7; Acts 5:36; 21:38) and James may also be speaking through the church members to their unbelieving neighbours in local communities, guilty of disruption and aggression in their home towns and villages.

It is also possible that our author may intend the saying in verse 2 to be interpreted in the light of Christ's teaching (so important to him) in Matthew 5:21,22 (compare 1 John 3:15) and that the wars here are 'private quarrels and lawsuits, social rivalries and factions and religious controversies' (Plummer). The words used here to depict fighting and warfare were also employed elsewhere to describe verbal battles and personal disputes. In the light of earlier teaching on the tongue, this is the most likely interpretation. The people who misuse their tongues in addressing men do the same in approaching God; they do not ask him for the right things (3), whilst others are totally prayerless (2b). This kind of conduct is the behaviour typical of the man whose horizons are confined to this world; it is a form of life which has no spiritual dimension at all. But it is not simply life without God; it is a life of enmity towards him (4).

THOUGHT: Those who 'fight' their neighbours are really at war with God. This passage should certainly be read alongside similar teaching in 1 John, especially 2:15–17; 3:11–18; 4:7–12. In love with the world, 'unfaithful creatures' (literally, adulteresses) do not reverence the peace-loving purposes of their Creator.

4:5–10 More grace

Today's reading begins with a rather difficult verse to interpret. We are not sure what passage in 'the scripture' James has in mind here (5). Hosea 11:8 has been suggested, though Exodus 20:5 is most likely, and it could mean that although by their worldliness men make themselves God's enemies, he does not easily abandon them, but *grieves* over their misconduct and *gives* (6) the grace sufficient for every circumstance of life. The reference in verse 5 to 'spirit' may refer to the human spirit or the indwelling Holy Spirit (1 Cor. 6:19; 2 Cor. 6:16). With understandable exaggeration, Erasmus said that there are 'waggon-loads of interpretations of this passage'. See C. L. Mitton's commentary for a helpful summary of the most likely possibilities. The NEB translation uses the term 'envious desires' to refer to man's evil inclinations. The RSV rendering, which emphasises God's holy yearning or longing, seems to fit more naturally into the context here (see Phil. 1:8; 1 Pet. 2:2, where the same word is used). 'What James means is that God is the jealous lover, who will brook no rival in the human heart, and that he must receive from us a love which is beyond all earthly devotion' (Barclay).

James makes it clear that God does something more than grieve; he offers help to his rebellious children, sufficient (2 Cor. 12:9), abundant (Rom. 5:20) and increasing (6) grace, or, if we follow the NEB translation of verse 5, grace greater than the downward pull of man's 'envious desires'. James follows this promise of grace for the humble with ten short exhortations which emphasise the necessity of submission to God, opposition to the enemy, communion with God, penitence and humility. It all stands in stark opposition to the arrogant, self-confident worldliness described in the earlier passages of this letter. Readers with a sense of humour need not feel condemned by the teaching of verse 9. Mitton has reminded us that what is rebuked here is 'the flippant laughter of careless unconcern in the presence of facts which more properly should induce grief and remorse'. This scholar points out that 'laughter can have great healing powers, to relieve inward stress and tension, and to ease strained personal relationships . . . But very easily laughter can become poisoned with bitterness and uncleanness . . . Very often, also, it becomes an instrument of cruelty, so that while others laugh someone who is the butt of the joke is embarrassed and humiliated.'

THOUGHT: Alongside the Ten Commands in this passage, there are three promises. The enemy will flee (7). God will draw near (8). He will exalt us (10). But note that these promises all have conditions attached to them.

4:11–17 Kind towards all

James knows that more is necessary than penitence and humility before God (5–10); the man truly surrendered to God (7) and in communion with him (8) will be kind to his neighbour. A man cannot be humble before God and arrogant before men; love for God demands love for others as both this letter and 1 John frequently emphasise. The word James uses in verse 11, 'to speak evil against', literally means 'to run somebody down'; loveless criticism is one of the tongue's worst sins. The 'law' here is doubtless the royal law of love he has mentioned earlier (2:8) and these verses are probably another echo of the teaching of Jesus (Matt. 7:1,2 as well as Lev. 19 with its sins of the tongue). Unkind conversation about others always comes back on ourselves anyway. One of James's contemporaries, Seneca, said that malice 'drinks up one half of its own poison'. The man or woman who arrogantly sits in judgement, constantly criticising others, is guilty of appalling self-exaltation. Jesus warned us against such unspiritual activity. 'Spiritual pride is very apt to suspect others; whereas an humble saint is most jealous of himself, he is as suspicious of nothing in the world as he is of his own heart. The spiritually proud person is apt to find fault with other saints, that they are low in grace; and to be much in observing how cold and dead they are; and being quick to discern and take notice of their deficiencies. But the eminently humble Christian has so much to do at home . . . that he is not apt to be very busy with other hearts' (Jonathan Edwards).

James is concerned about presumptuous speech (13–16) as well as destructive talk. The arrogant man forgets that his life is as brief as the morning mist, or a puff of smoke which quickly disappears (compare similar expressions regarding the brevity of man's life in Job 7:7,9; Ps. 102:11; 103:15), and makes all his decisions without any reference to God. Yet even a reverential submissive attitude towards him and a recognition of his sovereignty are not enough if we are not eagerly employed in practical love towards his children. If we know from the royal law that we are to love our neighbour and we remain selfishly unconcerned, that is a serious sin of omission. Sin is not only lawlessness (1 John 3:4); it is also lovelessness.

QUESTION: In the teaching of Jesus men who knew the law well were condemned for doing nothing when there was such rich opportunity for loving care (Luke 7:44–46; 10:31,32; 16:19–31; 18:22–25). Do we merely listen to the word?

5:1–6 Rich, empty and condemned

Today's passage is strikingly reminiscent not only of the teaching of Jesus (Matt. 6:19,20; Luke 6:24) but also of the eighth-century prophets where this theme of oppression by the greedy and loveless rich is taken up with such pressing urgency (Amos 2:6,7; 3:15; 4:1; 5:12; 6:4–6; 8:4–6; Mic. 6:8–15; 7:2,3; Isa. 1:21–23; 3:13–26). As in 4:1–4, James may be using this opportunity to address the rich people in the local communities where these churches were set, but he is also at pains here as earlier in the letter (2:1–7) to warn wealthy Christians (compare 1:10) of the danger of greed. Concerned about improving their bank balance, greedy people utterly lacking in generosity also increase the list of sins for which they will ultimately be judged (1,3b; compare Rom. 2:5). It is better to invest in present compassion than future condemnation. On verse 4 note how Leviticus 19, often in the background of James's teaching about love, has something to say about the responsibility of employers (compare Deut. 24:14,15; Mal. 3:5). Unjust landowners may be deaf to the plea of their deprived tenants and workers, but God hears every sigh. 'The Almighty God has an *ear* for the cries of the oppressed, and He makes their cause His own, so that they have a strong Defender indeed' (Alexander Ross).

The fact that these avaricious materialists have 'killed the righteous man' (6) suggests that the main offenders were unbelievers. Note that James does not encourage aggressive resistance against such tyranny (6b); that is an important observation in the light of contemporary theologies of 'liberation', some of which either condone or actively promote violent measures in their opposition to injustice. Any serious inequality or deprivation is certainly contrary to God's purpose of love for all mankind (read Ronald Sider's books, *Rich Christians in an Age of Hunger* and *Christ and Violence*), but at a time when forceful resistance to oppression was characteristic of some political zealots, James does not believe it to be a characteristically Christian response. This certainly does not mean that in our contemporary situation we do nothing about injustice and oppression; one must pray, work, plead, campaign and give. But to kill or destroy in order to achieve the good is to use the world's methods for God's work; it will not honour him nor will it heal the deep wounds of injustice or cruelty.

TWO IMPORTANT QUESTIONS: What proportion of your regular Christian giving is allocated to work among the world's hungry? In what way could you encourage your local church to do something sacrificial on a regular basis to support Christian ministry to starving people overseas?

5:7–12 Steadfastness and dependence

The constantly repeated appeal, 'brethren' (7,9,10,12,19), puts these readers clearly in contrast with the godless materialists primarily addressed in the preceding verses. Just as the greedy and ungenerous rich are awaiting the judgement (1,3b), so are the patient 'brethren' (7,8b,9b). There is little point in the farmer getting angry or irritable because the harvest is delayed. Likewise, the believer will not, in adversity, chafe restlessly under his burden either by blaming God or by grumbling against his neighbour (9). He will be 'patient', which means not only passively 'sticking it' (because you can do nothing else), but actively 'sticking at it' (because God gives us the stability and persistence necessary). James reminds his readers of two examples of steadfastness: the Old Testament prophets (10, fitting in view of 4:1–6, a 'prophetic' type of condemnation such as incurred a good deal of wrath among the contemporaries of men like Amos and Jeremiah, e.g. Amos 7:12,13; Jer. 11:18–23; 20:1,2,7–12) and an Old Testament patriarch, Job (11). Those who are steadfast are happy in the present (11) and confident about the future (8).

His main concern, however, is not to illustrate courageous stability from the past, but encourage it in the present, and he does so by reminding these churches of some great truths about the Lord: his promised return (8b), searching, impending justice (9), sovereign goodness (11b, 'you have seen the purpose of the Lord', i.e. for Job) and merciful compassion (11c). Those who know his worth will never resist his will. In the closing verse of today's passage James returns again to the teaching of Jesus (Matt. 5:33–37). In distressing circumstances people can sometimes be guilty of profane speech. It is vain and flippant language which is being condemned here. Men will be judged not only for their godless selfishness (1–6) but also for their vain, blasphemous or totally useless conversation (Matt. 12:36). A Christian's words should be both dependable and profitable. Writing about Christian behaviour in the late second century, Clement of Alexandria maintained that the true Christian 'has little temptation to lying and swearing' for 'how could one who has once for all proved himself faithful, make himself unfaithful so as to stand in need of an oath?' Clement insists that the believer's word is trustworthy and reliable. A Christian 'shows the faithfulness of his promise by unfailing steadfastness both of life and speech'.

THOUGHT: For the Christian, it is not enough to *avoid* unhelpful and unkind conversation (James 3). The New Testament calls us to positive action as well. Believers recognise the necessity of encouraging, constructive and edifying speech. The prophets 'who spoke in the name of the Lord' (10) did not only correct faults. They declared truth and offered hope.

5:13–20 Let him sing praise

The concluding section of our letter deals with a number of issues of natural concern to a local church – prayer in adversity, worship in jubilation, the healing of the sick, mutual confession of sin and the restoration of penitent offenders. Note Paul's insistence on praise (Eph. 5:19; Rom. 15:9). The helpful counsel offered to the physically unwell (14,15) has been the unfortunate battle-ground of needless controversy. It does not support the contention of the dogmatic faith healer who insists that every sick person must be physically healed *if* there is enough faith (with consequent depression if healing does not come); what about sick people in the New Testament who do not appear to have been instantaneously healed (1 Tim. 5:23; 2 Tim. 4:20)? Neither does this important statement about healing support the Roman Catholic 'sacrament' of extreme unction which, as Luther pointed out in his *Babylonish Captivity*, is preparation for death, not for restoration of life as James intends. The advice offered here surely emphasises the local church's corporate responsibility to pray for *and with* sick people, utter reliance on the Lord, the necessity of ensuring that the sick person (or anyone else) is not harbouring unforgiven sin, e.g. resentment, bitterness – an important recognition of the close relationship between body and mind or spirit. Verse 16 further recognises the importance of the accepting and forgiving community of love. Its teaching must be interpreted in the light of other Scripture (e.g. Eph. 4:29; 5:11,12), therefore not as authority for 'auricular confession', or as encouragement for public grovelling over our misdeeds. Rather, such confession should serve as a reminder that corporate prayer, and the forgiveness that God has given can be healing and spiritually restorative factors in our lives. Constancy in prayer, whether we are deeply depressed or radiantly happy (13), reminds James of the prophet Elijah, not, as some first-century Jewish writers were suggesting, a mythical hero, utterly detached from life, but 'a man like us' (J. B. Phillips). He prayed fervently, sacrificially (he did not know about Cherith when he prayed for famine, 1 Kings 17:1–7), confidently ('then he prayed again') and effectively ('earth brought forth'). The letter closes (19,20) with an appeal to *all* members ('some one', not just leaders) to bring back those who have wandered, knowing that the restored sinner will be both immediately forgiven and ultimately saved.

THOUGHT: Commenting on verse 13, Alexander Ross has said that Christians 'can sing praise in the most trying circumstances, sometimes even in a prison at midnight (Acts 16:25), but how many there are who, in the noontide of their greatest prosperity, forget to give thanks to the Giver of all good.'

Questions for further study and discussion on James 3–5

1. Every Christian's tongue is exposed to some particular temptation – criticism, gossip, hypocrisy and pride are but a few of the more obvious ones. Examine your own life in the light of this teaching in James. Have the courage to identify your failures and consider ways in which your tongue could be even more helpfully used in the local church and beyond it.

2. Recognising with James that 'we all make many mistakes' (3:2), which do you consider to be the *three* most serious ones in the last three chapters of the letter?

3. What is meant by worldliness (4:4) in the New Testament? How would you define it in today's world?

4. Are there dangers in constantly qualifying all we plan with the actual words, 'If the Lord wills' (4:15)? Does James insist here that we *say* those words every time we make statements about anything in the future? If he is encouraging something else less easy than the utterance of a pious cliché, what might that be?

5. In the light of this letter's teaching about care and prayer, what can be done in your local church about (*a*) the needs of the hungry overseas and (*b*) the lonely in your immediate locality?

6. What are the special dangers and temptations of leadership (3:1)? What does that say to us as leaders, and as supporters?

7. How would you exemplify, for a modern reader, the two types of wisdom of 3:13–18?

8. What is your reaction to James's attack on the rich? Now try to put yourself in the position of the many millions living at or below subsistence level – how would *they* expect *you* to react?